Volunteers of America®

OKLAHOMA

Presents this book to:

Mounds Public Library

www.voaok.org

THE INSIDE TRACK LIBRARY

Banking

THE INSIDE TRACK LIBRARY

Banking

Nancy Dunnan

SILVER BURDETT PRESS

Published by Silver Burdett Press, Inc., a division of Simon & Schuster, Inc., Prentice Hall Bldg., Englewood Cliffs, NJ 07632.

Created and produced by: Blackbirch Graphics, Inc.

Project Editor: Emily Easton
Designer: Cynthia Minichino

Manufactured in the United States of America

10 9 8 7 6 5 4 3 2 1

Library of Congress Cataloging-in-Publication Data

Dunnan, Nancy.
   Banking/Nancy Dunnan
   (Inside track library)
   Summary: Surveys the history and functions of banks and discusses how to manage your money.
   1. Banks and banking—Juvenile literature. 2. Finance, Personal-Juvenile literatre. [1. Banks and banking. 2. Finance, Personal.] I. Title. II. Series: Dunnan, Nancy. Inside track library.
HG1609.D86 1990
332.1—dc20
ISBN 0-382-09917-6 (lib. bdg.)
ISBN 0-382-24028-6 (pbk.)

                                        90-35429
                                            CIP
                                            AC

(Frontispiece)
Boy reviews his bank book at teller's window.

CONTENTS

Suburban banks bring their services to residential areas.

1

WHAT IS A BANK?

You probably pass by a **bank** on your way to school, or when you go shopping or visiting friends. You may have spent time inside a bank with your parents, or perhaps you have done business with one on your own.

All of us take banks very much for granted, yet they are one of the most important institutions in our lives. Every day, each one of us either uses a bank or is affected by someone who does. The more you know about how they work, the more control you will have over your finances and the easier it will be to accumulate wealth.

How Banks Work

A bank is really a business that takes in money and keeps it for the owner or customer. Very often banks pay **interest** to the **depositor** of the money and then in turn lend out this same money to others,

Bank: A financial institution that keeps money for others, makes loans, and offers other money-related services.

Interest: The cost of using money; when you borrow money from a bank you must pay the bank for that money. The amount you pay is called interest and is expressed as a percent, such as 8 percent.

Depositor: A person or business who puts money in a bank.

9

Loan: *Letting out or renting of money by a lender to a borrower with the understanding that the money will be paid back.*

Checks: *An order to pay money drawn on a checking account that is payable upon presentation by the person or business the order is made out to.*

Credit card: *A small plastic card, issued by banks, stores, and businesses to customers, allowing them to charge their purchases and pay for them later.*

Barter: *Direct exchange of one good for another without the use of money.*

charging them interest for the use of the money. This transaction is known as a **loan**. Banks also aid in the exchange or movement of money between people and businesses by offering various services such as **checks** and **credit cards**.

Banks, like any other business, want to make a profit. They do so by charging customers for checks and other services and by lending customers' money to borrowers at higher interest rates than they pay depositors.

Before There Was Money

You may think that money has been around forever—but it hasn't. Before money and banks were available to everyone, people used the **barter** system. If you were a farmer, for example, you might exchange your eggs or corn with someone who had a supply of nails. However, a farmer who wanted nails had to find a nailmaker who wanted eggs at the same time. This was not always easy. This "double coincidence" of wants, inherent in the barter system, eventually led to the use of money. When the same type of money is used by a large number of people—say, an entire country—the exchange of goods and services is not only simpler but it's also faster. Paying the nailmaker with money is much more convenient than finding a nailmaker who wants your dozen eggs when you want nails. Our ability to use money, however, depends upon everyone being willing to accept it as the medium of exchange.

What Is Money?

Money can be any prized thing that a group agrees upon. The American Indians used beads. The Inuit, or Eskimo, used fish hooks. Shells, stones, furs, and grain have also been used as money in certain

Stone wheel used for money by inhabitants of the Yap Islands.

areas. The Yap Islanders of the Pacific used massive stone "money" wheels until World War II. Today industrialized societies use coins, paper bills, and checks. Money, then, is that which is a generally acceptable medium of exchange.

Money has another advantage: When the nailmaker trades nails for eggs, he must use the eggs within a certain time period, or they will spoil. On the other hand, if he sells his nails for money, he doesn't have to spend all of it immediately, or ever. It won't spoil. Money can be set aside, saved, and used later.

The three key advantages of money are: 1) as a means to buy things and settle debts; 2) as a store of value when you hold on to it; and 3) as a standard of value or a unit of value so you can compare prices between various goods and services.

When we use money instead of bartering, money becomes precious and requires a place for safekeeping. That place, of course, is the bank.

Banking in Ancient Times

No one really knows what the world's first bank was, although types of banks existed in ancient times. The sanctuary at Delphi in Greece was used to store gold **bullion** and other valuables. In Athens in the sixth and fifth centuries B.C., individual merchants accepted deposits of coin and gold bullion for safekeeping. Moneychangers in the Temple at Jerusalem are described in the New Testament. They exchanged coins for visiting merchants. In the second and first centuries B.C., Romans used money shops to pay taxes and settle other bills with creditors. The Romans also used an assignment or "attributio" to settle debts, rather like our present-day checks. The money dealers, or "argentarii," also changed money and dealt in interest.

Bullion: Refined gold or silver in bulk, rather than in the form of coins.

Scholars generally agree that the word "bank" comes from the Italian "banco" for bench, because in Italy during medieval times, money traders sat at benches in the marketplace to meet their customers. The Italians also gave us our word for **bankruptcy**: when a money merchant ran into financial trouble, his bench was broken to indicate that his business had failed.

Bankruptcy: When a person or a business declares they are unable to pay their bills and other debts.

It is somewhat easier to trace the origin of money than that of banks. Because money is generally more acceptable to a group of people if it is durable or lasting, metal money was popular from the earliest times. The Egyptians produced the first metal money in about 2,500 B.C. They made money in the shape of rings. About 400 years later, the Chinese were using gold cubes as money. Then, in 700 B.C. in Lydia (today, western Turkey), the first metal coins were **struck**. Made from an **alloy** of gold and silver called electrum, these crudely inscribed coins were bean-shaped pellets.

Struck/strike: To impress a design by stamping or pressing it onto a surface, in this case, making a coin.

Credit for the idea of paper money goes to the Babylonians, who wrote bills and receipts on clay tablets. Marco Polo brought back news to Europe that the Chinese Emperor, Kubla Khan, issued paper money made of mulberry bark that bore his seal. In fact, the oldest surviving example of paper

Alloy: A blend or mixture of two or more metals.

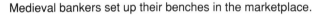
Medieval bankers set up their benches in the marketplace.

money today is the Kwan, a Chinese note from the Ming Dynasty, towards the end of the fourteenth century. It is about the size of a piece of typewriting paper.

During the Middle Ages, when people began traveling farther distances, coins faded from popularity, not only because they were so heavy, but because merchants and crusaders feared being robbed. Travelers began leaving their coins with goldsmiths for safekeeping and taking receipts with them. These receipts had little value to robbers since they could be exchanged only for coins with a designated goldsmith in another city. Eventually people used the receipts themselves to pay debts rather than withdraw the actual coins from their goldsmith's shop. These receipts were in effect paper money. People also began paying bills by writing a letter to their goldsmith, instructing him to give coins to the holder or bearer of the letter. These letters were an early form of today's checks.

> A banker is a fellow who lends his umbrella when the sun is shining and wants it back the minute it begins to rain.
>
> —Mark Twain, 1893

Banking in Early America

Before the Revolutionary War, banks as we know them simply did not exist in America. That's because coinage of money was the prerogative of the king of England and British laws limited the amount of coins that could be brought into the colonies. The few coins the colonists owned were used to import the many basic necessities they needed. Because they had so little currency, the colonists were forced to run their world by exchanging goods through the barter system. At first they used Indian wampum as money. Gunpowder, bullets, tobacco, grain, fish, and furs were also used.

Massachusetts, tired and angered by this inefficient system, defied the Crown and became the first British colony to make its own coin. In 1652 it

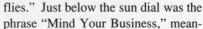

THE FIRST NATIONAL COIN

The first national coin was struck in 1787, when Congress asked James Jarvis to make copper one-cent coins. One side of the coin was decorated with a chain of thirteen links encircling the motto "We Are One." The other side had a sun dial, the noonday sun, and the word "fugio," meaning "time 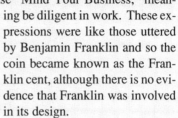 flies." Just below the sun dial was the phrase "Mind Your Business," meaning be diligent in work. These expressions were like those uttered by Benjamin Franklin and so the coin became known as the Franklin cent, although there is no evidence that Franklin was involved in its design.

began striking the pine tree shilling in a **mint** located in Boston. Several types of shillings as well as six- and three-pence pieces were also produced by this mint until the English closed it down in 1686.

Four years later, in 1690, Massachusetts issued paper money to its soldiers returning from their unsuccessful seige of Quebec. Because they lost the battle, these men were not entitled to booty or pay. Hundreds of them, hungry, tired, and beaten, were nearly mutinous. To salvage the terrible situation, the colony gave bills of credit or **promissory notes**. These notes were the first paper money in America—and in fact for the entire British Empire. Other colonies soon began issuing their own paper money, too, but some issued far too much, causing it to become worth only a small fraction of its original **face value**.

As trade with the West Indies developed, Spanish eight reales pieces were widely used. Known as "pieces of eight," the colonists often cut these coins to make change. Half a coin was known as "four bits" and a quarter section as "two bits."

Mint: A place where legal coins are manufactured.

Promissory note: A written promise to pay a stated sum of money to the payee upon demand at any time in the future.

Face value: Sometimes called par value. The dollar value of a bond, note, or mortgage as stated on its certificate.

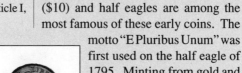

THE U.S. MINT

"The Congress shall have the power . . . To Coin Money."
(Constitution of the United States, Article I, Section 8)

On April 2, 1792, Congress created the Mint and authorized that it be built in what was then the nation's capital, Philadelphia. President George Washington appointed David Rittenhouse, a leading scientist, as the first director. Under Rittenhouse, the Mint produced its first coins—11,178 individual copper cents were

issued. Soon thereafter it began issuing gold and silver coins. The gold eagles ($10) and half eagles are among the most famous of these early coins. The motto "E Pluribus Unum" was first used on the half eagle of 1795. Minting from gold and silver continued until 1933. Then, during the Great Depression, the Mint stopped producing gold coins. In 1965, a silver crisis ended the use of silver in quarters and dimes, although half dollars were composed of 40 percent silver until 1970.

Inventories: A business's raw materials, supplies, and items in the process of being made as well as finished goods on hand, often in a factory, warehouse, garage, or barn.

Collateral: Specific property that a borrower pledges as security against repayment of a loan. The lender can sell the collateral if the borrower fails to repay the loan.

Land banks were also established in several of the colonies. These were set up by individual groups of farmers and merchants who banded together, pledging their property, such as land, **inventories**, stores, and homes, as security or **collateral** against paper money the bank would issue to them through loans. By 1750, land banks existed in all colonies except Virginia, and they were extremely successful. They were a source of low-interest credit, sorely needed for agricultural expansion. They also built up purchasing power among the colonists.

Not surprisingly, the British government found all these banking moves threatening, and considered them to be an attempt by the colonists to undermine the authority of the Crown. And so the British banished all efforts by the colonists to issue money by passing several laws, the most severe being the so-called Currency Act of 1751, which applied to the New England states. It stated that no new land banks could be created, no paper money could be made **legal tender**, and all bills were to be withdrawn from circulation.

Legal tender: *Money that the government requires a creditor to accept in discharge of debts.*

The colonists, however, were a feisty group and simply refused to obey this and other laws they found too harsh and stifling. The Currency Act and other British rules only served to further alienate the colonists from the British Crown and eventually led to the Revolutionary War.

The war created another monetary problem. Facing huge wartime expenses without the power to tax the people, the Continental Congress, less than a week after the Battle of Bunker Hill, authorized $2,000,000 of paper money. Because it did not have taxing authority, the Congress could not redeem these notes in gold, silver, or **specie**, or make them legal tender. It recommended, instead, that they be redeemed by the individual states. The states paid little heed to the suggestion and so by 1780 the notes fell to 1/40th of their original face value. From this particular situation came the term "not worth a continental," which means that a person or thing is absolutely worthless.

Specie: *Coined money as opposed to paper money.*

Currency: *Any form of money that is generally circulated. Although it technically includes both paper and coin, bankers tend to use the term for paper money only.*

The nearly nonexistent value of the nation's first **currency** created a bitter feeling toward paper money that lasted for many years.

THE FIRST U.S. INFLATION

Because continental money quickly became nearly worthless, prices for most things rose to unheard of heights. By January 1782, it took $100 in paper money to buy $1 in silver. Other items also soared in price, if payment was in paper money:

- a pair of shoes   cost $ 100
- a bushel of corn   cost $ 40
- a pound of tea   cost $ 90
- a barrel of flour   cost $1,575

When America gained its independence, the colonists continued to fight—not with the British but each other—over whether or not the federal government should back a **central bank** to regulate money. The fight lasted for the next 100 years. Alexander Hamilton, our first Secretary of the Treasury, persuaded the first Congress to create a central bank. It was called the First Bank of the United States and it opened its doors in 1791, despite the vigorous opposition by Thomas Jefferson and his supporters, who distrusted strong central control.

The Bank of the United States had a twenty-year **charter**. It was a private corporation and issued its own notes, which were **backed** by its gold and silver holdings. It also exerted control in another way—it limited the amount of money that **state-chartered banks** could issue. Opponents of the Bank, who thought it had too much power over the national economy, managed to prevent its charter from being renewed and the Bank closed its doors in 1811.

Then, during the War of 1812, the state-chartered banks were unable to provide enough financial support to help the government pay for the war, so in 1816, Congress authorized a second central bank. Andrew Jackson vigorously fought the Second Bank because he felt it hampered states' rights. He vetoed extending its charter and its doors were closed in 1836.

After the Second Bank folded, notes were issued by state-chartered, private banks. These notes were redeemable in gold or silver, which meant the banks had to keep a reserve of precious metal on hand to meet redemptions. Each state bank designed its own notes, so there were many different sizes and colors. By the 1860s, an estimated 8,000 banks

THE WILDCATS

In the early 1800s, America had many honest local banks, but some, called "wildcat banks," intentionally deceived the public. These dishonest banks were nicknamed wildcats because they were located in places so far from civilization that it was said that wildcats roamed up to their doors. Banking regulators seldom made it out to examine these banks, a fact some bankers took advantage of.

At the time, bankers were required to keep a certain amount of precious metal on hand to redeem notes from customers and pay out coins upon request. The honest ones often put their gold and silver reserve vaults in plain view of the customers, but the less scrupulous ones found a way around this: they threw a layer of coins on top of a keg of nails, fooling the public and bank examiners into thinking they had more precious metal in reserve than actually was the case.

were circulating different notes. Counterfeiters found it easy to issue bogus money with so many varieties and designs in circulation. The state bank notes were not always accepted in all parts of the country. A cotton merchant from the South doing business in New York, for example, might find his money worth less or even nothing in the North. In fact, much of the money issued at this time circulated at big **discounts** from face value. Not surprisingly, many Americans developed a strong distrust of paper money at this time. They believed only in gold or silver.

Discount: When a security or note sells below its face value.

To help resolve this problem of distrust, the federal government itself issued paper money to finance the Civil War. These noninterest-paying demand notes were called *greenbacks,* because of their color. They were redeemable by the government in coin on demand when presented at certain banks. Greenbacks were technically the first official paper currency accepted as money across the nation.

But banking problems continued to plague the country until 1913, when the Federal Reserve Act was passed. We'll learn how this act led to a more stable, unified banking system—the one we operate with today—in the next chapter.

Rich men die but banks are immortal.

—Wendell Phillips, 1863

BUTCH CASSIDY AND THE SUNDANCE KID

Among the most romantic of the bank robbers of the old West were Butch Cassidy and the Sundance Kid. Their famous story, immortalized by Paul Newman and Robert Redford in the movie of the same name, is particularly unique and intriguing because of their great loyalty to each other.

Butch Cassidy was born Robert Le-Roy Parker on a farm in Circleville, Utah, one of ten children. He changed his last name to Cassidy because of his fondness for Mike Cassidy, a neighbor who taught him how to shoot, rustle cattle, and rob banks. He earned the nickname Butch while working as a butcher in Rock Springs, Wyoming. But Butch hated legitimate work and when Mike Cassidy, head of his own gang of oulaws, disappeared, Butch took over. He was a natural leader.

In 1894 he was arrested for stealing cattle and spent two years in the Wyoming State Prison. While there he heard tales about a fabulous mountain hideout for gunmen and bandits in Colorado called Hole-in-the-Wall. When he was released from prison in 1896, Butch headed there to recruit a new gang. Hole-in-the-Wall is also where he met Harry Longbaugh.

Harry was known as the Sundance Kid from his time in the jail in Sundance, Wyoming. Although he wore only one gun, he had the fastest draw anyone had seen at the time. The two men became great friends. Their first big robbery together took place in July 1901 when they hit a train, the Great Northern Flyer, near Malta, Montana. Sundance sat in one of the coaches until others in the gang ordered the engineers to stop the train. Then he ran up and down the passenger cars, firing his pistol into the air

and shouting: "Keep your heads inside!" Butch jumped onto the train and set off a massive charge of dynamite to open the safe. The take was more than $40,000.

A posse of a hundred men chased Butch and Sundance but the outlaws knew the terrain and managed to ecape to Texas, where they rested at Fannie Porter's brothel in Fort Worth. In Fort Worth, Butch took up bicycle riding and Sundance took up with Etta Place, a beautiful school teacher who loved excitement. The Pinkerton Detective Agency, which had been pursuing the two men for years, got wind of the outlaws' whereabouts. So, Butch, Sundance, and Etta headed for Bolivia where they continued their career. Etta acted as scout for the two men, going into one bank after another, theoretically to open an account, but in reality to case the place, count the number of guards, and then report back to Butch and Sundance.

In 1907, Etta asked to go home. Sundance accompanied her back to the States, first to New York and then to Denver. One night, not long after they arrived in Denver, he got drunk, shot up a saloon, and left his schoolteacher-turned-robber forever. He headed back to Bolivia and his old friend, Butch. But their bank robbing days were numbered. The story goes that the two men were trapped by soldiers near San Vincente, Bolivia, in 1908. Outnumbered, they dove for their rifles, which were on the other side of a large open patio. The soldiers fired as they ran. Sundance was hit immediately. He fell and died in the dust. When Butch saw that his friend was dead, he turned his six gun on himself and joined him.

Some historians say that the tale ended differently: that Cassidy survived the ambush, went back to Utah, where he visited his family in 1929, then aimlessly roamed the countryside, dying around 1937 in Johnny, Nevada.

The Hole-in-the-Wall Gang assembled in Fort Worth in 1901 to have a portrait made "as a good joke." Seated at right is Butch Cassidy and at far left is Sundance Kid.

BONDS FOR VICTORY

BUY WAR BONDS

Bonds helped finance the U.S. Treasury during World War II.

THE FLOW OF MONEY

After the break with England, Americans remained suspicious of centralized control of almost any kind and for this reason the U.S. was the last major industrial nation to establish a central bank. Even at the beginning of the 20th century, most banks were still keeping relatively little cash on hand. Small country banks deposited their cash reserves in larger banks which then, in turn, deposited them in city banks. This pyramiding of money often led to disaster. Bad business conditions or poor farming crops often caused depositors to panic and line up outside their banks, waiting for hours if necessary to withdraw their money. Often local banks were unable to meet such widespread demand for cash and so they called upon the bigger banks. If their vaults were also low on reserves, the withdrawal requests could not be met, and the banks simply closed their doors. Sometimes people lost all their money.

The problem was exacerbated at the time by the absence of enforceable government regulations over the supply of money. So, instead of a central authority, thousands of individual banks, each operating in a small geographical area, determined how much money there was in the country. The money supply, in fact, was subject to quick changes as the country went through "boom and bust" periods. A series of bank failures resulted in the famous bank panic of 1907, when millions of depositors lost their savings and the economy went into a nosedive.

The Federal Reserve System

The National Monetary Commission, set up to remedy this chaotic situation, recommended creation of the Federal Reserve System. President Woodrow Wilson signed the Federal Reserve Act in December 1913. The act required all national banks to become members. State banks could become members but were not required to join.

The Federal Reserve Act created a central banking system consisting of twelve regional Reserve banks located throughout the country. Each of these banks acts as a central banker for the private banks in its area, holding money reserves, providing cash, granting loans to member banks and performing other services. Each district is designated by a number and the corresponding letter:

> There have been three great inventions since the beginning of time: fire, the wheel, and central banking.
>
> —Will Rogers, 1920

1	Boston	A	7	Chicago	G
2	New York	B	8	St. Louis	H
3	Philadelphia	C	9	Minneapolis	I
4	Cleveland	D	10	Kansas City	J
5	Richmond	E	11	Dallas	K
6	Atlanta	F	12	San Francisco	L

The first U.S. Mint in Philadelphia.

There are also a number of Federal Reserve Bank branches. Call the one nearest your home; many district and branch banks have tours.

Buffalo	New Orleans	El Paso
Cincinnati	Detroit	Houston
Pittsburgh	Little Rock	San Antonio
Baltimore	Louisville	Los Angeles
Charlotte	Memphis	Portland
Birmingham	Helena	Salt Lake City
Jacksonville	Denver	Seattle
Nashville	Oklahoma City	

Each Reserve Bank issues its own paper money, called "Federal Reserve Notes." We call them bills: we have $1, $5, $10, $20, $50, and $100 bills in circulation today. It costs about 2 1/2 cents to produce each note. The Federal Reserve Banks issue notes according to the needs of their area. You can tell which bank issued any bill by looking at the Bank Seal, printed in black at the left of the portrait and showing the name of the bank in the circle. This cash, plus the money in checking accounts, constitutes today's definition of the money supply.

How Money Moves Around the Country

When your bank needs more coins and bills to meet customer demand, it can order this cash from its

Federal Reserve Bank or branch. Public demand
for money varies. For example, during the Christmas season, more people want cash for shopping.
The Fed will ship the money by armored car or
registered mail to the bank. To meet demand by
member banks for cash, the Fed keeps a large
supply of bills and coins in its vaults.

Another situation in which a bank needs extra
money is when a customer wants to withdraw a
huge amount. The Fed will loan banks money to
cover such needs. The bank must pay the Fed
interest, called the **discount rate**, to borrow this
money. These loans are often made by "Fedwire,"
an electronic communications network that transfers
information, funds, and securities throughout the
country. For example, if a business person in San
Francisco needs a large amount of money for an
important business acquisition from the firm's
corporate headquarters in New York, the home
office notifies its bank, which in turn calls the New
York Federal Reserve Bank. The New York Federal Reserve Bank then wires the funds to the
Federal Reserve Bank in San Francisco which in
turns wires the money to the executive's local bank.

The Fed is also our government's bank. The
Fed handles so many checks each day that, laid
down end to end, they would stretch from New
York to Alaska.

The Federal Reserve System initially brought
much needed order to the chaotic world of banking.
It also helped finance World War I. The system
worked well until the stock market crashed in
October 1929, when plummeting stock prices
resulted in the failure of many banks. A severe
nationwide bank panic lasted until March 1933,
when President Franklin D. Roosevelt closed all
banks for four days. It was called a "bank holiday."

*Discount rate: The interest
rate charged by
Federal Reserve
Banks for lending
reserves to private
banks. The rate is
listed regularly in
the financial pages
of the newspaper.*

President Franklin D.
Roosevelt.

Headline after stock market crashed in October, 1929.

When the so-called holiday was over, only solvent banks—those with sufficient assets—re-opened their doors.

The Money Supply

Today the Federal Reserve has a great impact on our daily lives because it manages the nation's money supply. It is not involved in who gets money or how they spend it. But it does try to make certain the total amount in circulation in the country is right—not too much, not too little. It is responsible for seeing that banks do not create so much money that we have **inflation** or so little that we have a period of declining production and unemployment, known as a **recession**.

Inflation: An increase in the overall prices of goods and services.

If there is too much money, prices for the things we all buy increase. You may have heard a newscaster report that "the cost of living has gone up." He or she is talking about the fact that a dozen donuts, a new car, or a bicycle costs more today than it did a month or a year ago. This is called inflation.

Recession: A decline in the country's total output and economic activity that is generally accompanied by increased unemployment.

On the other hand, too little money in circulation can lead to unemployment. When many people are out of work and times are financially hard, it is called a recession.

To prevent inflation or recession, the Federal Reserve tries to keep spending in balance with the production of goods and services. Since the Fed has no control over production, it turns its efforts toward regulating the amount of money private citizens, businesses, and the government have to spend. It controls our money supply in three different ways. It can change the reserve requirements, change the discount rate, or take action through its open market operations by buying and selling government bonds. Let's look at all three.

1) *The reserves.* Many years ago, a bank's reserves consisted of gold and silver held in its vaults, but today's reserves are different. Now the Fed requires member banks to keep a fraction of their own deposits on reserve at a regional Federal Reserve Bank. By changing this reserve percentage, the Fed affects the ability of member banks to make loans to customers. For example, by raising the reserve requirement, the amount of money local banks have available to loan to customers is reduced. When banks have less to loan, they charge borrowers higher interest rates and so people borrow less and spend less.

2) *The discount rate.* The Fed also controls the flow of money by changing the discount rate, the rate it charges banks when it lends them money. When the discount rate is high, the Fed is trying to restrain the money supply. Low discount rates, on the other hand, make borrowing easier. Low discount rates ultimately lead to lower interest rates on loans for clients, thus encouraging borrowing. When borrowing is easier and cheaper, people spend more.

3) *Open market operations.* The Fed also buys U.S. government bonds, called **Treasuries**, thus increasing bank reserves, or sells them, reducing

> It is safer to keep your money in a reopened bank than under your mattress.
>
> —Franklin D. Roosevelt, 1933

Treasuries: Bonds, notes, and bills issued by the U.S. government and backed by its full faith and credit. These securities are considered the safest and highest quality available.

reserves. If the Fed wants to increase the money supply and provide banks with more reserves, it buys government bonds. The sellers of these bonds deposit the money they receive from selling their bonds into the banks. This increases the money reserves. With this influx of money, banks can increase their loans. If consumers and businesses then borrow and spend that borrowed money, output and employment theoretically will be stimulated.

Bank robber Willie Sutton.

If the Fed wants to reduce the money supply, it sells government Treasuries. Buyers withdraw money from their banks to pay for their purchases. This reduces the money supply.

Now let's see how the Fed reacts when faced with either inflation or a recession. When the price of goods and services begins to rise the Fed usually tightens lending and credit. People and businesses cut back on spending and using borrowed money. This in turn helps put total spending in balance with the production of goods and services. Prices then generally start to stabilize.

When Willie Sutton was asked by a reporter why he robbed banks he said: "That's where the money is."

When the country is headed toward or is in a recession and the number of unemployed people is on the rise, the Fed typically makes it easier for banks to increase their lending by reducing the discount rate and easing up on reserve requirements. This tends to lower rates and thus stimulate spending with borrowed money, increase total spending, and boost the level of production. As production rises, unemployed workers return to work.

So, even though individuals do not bank directly at any of the Federal Reserve Banks, the Fed has an important impact on all of us.

• *Who Runs the Federal Reserve?* Although Congress created the Federal Reserve, it does not run the system. Nor does the President of the United States. The Fed is, in fact, an independent

• The word "cash" comes from "kasu," the Chinese word for a small coin.

• The word "money" comes from the Roman goddess, Juno Moneto, who guarded the mint.

• The word "dollar" comes from a coin minted in Bohemia around 1518. These coins were called "thalers" throughout Europe. The word was anglicized in Shakespeare's time as "dollars."

U.S. Mint Adjusting Room.

• Alexander Hamilton and Thomas Jefferson, our first Secretary of the Treasury and Secretary of State, decided that the "dollar" should be the standard unit of value.

• In 1916, the Federal government actually laundered money. Dirty money was sent to Washington and if it was in good condition it was washed, ironed and reissued.

organization within the government. This keeps the job of managing the country's money supply separate from political pressure.

The Fed has a seven-member Board of Governors, with headquarters in Washington, D.C. The President of the United States appoints the members of the Board with consent of the Senate. Each of the twelve Federal Reserve Banks around the country has its own president and board of directors.

Although each regional Federal Reserve Bank is quite autonomous, they also work as a team to keep the economy stable and healthy.

Understanding Our Currency

Over the years, the United States has issued many different coins and paper money. Much of this old money is valuable today as a collectible or antique. You can read about collectibles in another book in this series. But now we will learn about the money we use today.

• ***What Our Paper Currency Looks Like.*** Our paper bills (officially called Federal Reserve Notes) are made or engraved by the U.S. Bureau of Engraving and Printing in Washington, D.C. This

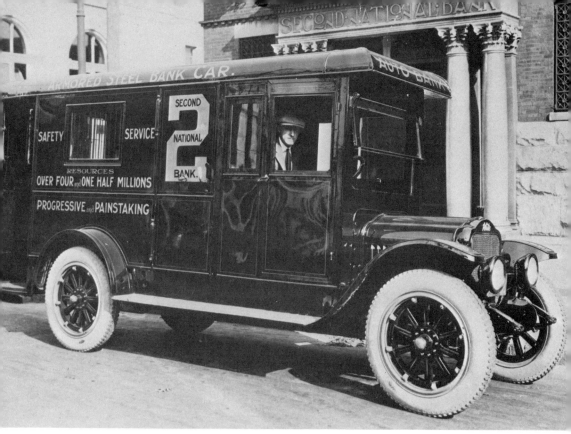

An Atlantic City bank used an Auto Bank to serve customers.

Bureau also designs and prints our postage stamps. Engravers cut the individual features of the design into steel dies. For security reasons, each feature, such as the portrait, ornaments, letters, and script, is done by a separate engraver. The intricate, lacy design and the borders are produced with a geometric lathe. Paper, specially produced by Crane & Co. of Dalton, Massachusetts, has been used since 1789. It contains no wood pulp; instead it is a blend of ragbond, cotton, and linen. The Bureau makes its own inks with secret formulas.

• *The serial number.* The serial number appears in two places on the face of all U.S. currency—in the upper right and lower left hand corners. Serial numbers are always eight digits. They also have a prefix letter and a suffix letter. The prefix letter corresponds to that in the Bank Seal and represents the Federal Reserve Bank that

Diagram of the Dollar Bill

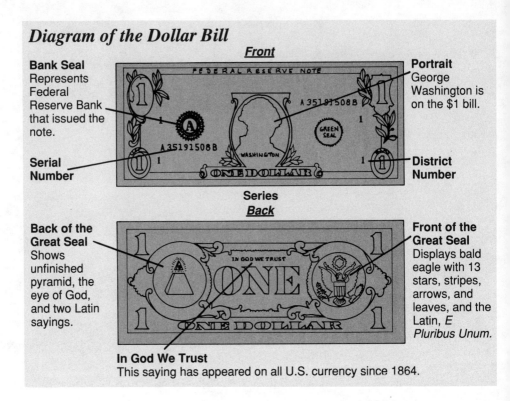

Front

Bank Seal
Represents Federal Reserve Bank that issued the note.

Serial Number

Portrait
George Washington is on the $1 bill.

District Number

Series

Back

Back of the Great Seal
Shows unfinished pyramid, the eye of God, and two Latin sayings.

Front of the Great Seal
Displays bald eagle with 13 stars, stripes, arrows, and leaves, and the Latin, *E Pluribus Unum.*

In God We Trust
This saying has appeared on all U.S. currency since 1864.

issued the note. For example, notes issued by the Kansas City Federal Reserve Bank, the tenth district, have the tenth letter of the alphabet—J—preceding the serial number. The notes are numbered in lots of 100,000,000. Because space is limited to eight numerals, a "star" is substituted for the 100,000,000th note. Each unit has a suffix letter beginning with A and following in alphabetical order through Z, omitting the letter O because it looks like a zero. For example, the serial number of the first run of any note for the Kansas City bank will read J-A; the second series will be J-B and so forth through J-Z.

• *Series.* This number is at the right of the portrait near the signature of the Secretary of the Treasury and shows the year the design was first used on a note. Sometimes a small change is made in the design that does not require a completely new engraving plate. This happens, for instance, when the Secretary of the Treasury changes. Then, the series year remains the same but a letter is added to indicate that the design differs somewhat from the previous printings of this particular issue.

• *Size* Until July 1929, our currency was 7.42 inches by 3.13 inches. These are called "old, large-size" or "blanket" bills. Since 1929, the size has been 6.14 inches by 2.61 inches. It is easier to handle and less expensive to produce.

• *Portraits and Emblems* These are currently or recently in use:

Denomination	Face	Reverse Side
$ 1	Washington	Ornate One and U.S. Seal
2	Jefferson	Painting*
5	Lincoln	Lincoln Memorial
10	Hamilton	U.S. Treasury
20	Jackson	White House
50	Grant	U.S. Capitol
100	Franklin	Independence Hall
**500	McKinley	Ornate Five Hundred
**1,000	Cleveland	Ornate One Thousand
**5,000	Madison	Ornate Five Thousand
**10,000	Chase	Ornate Ten Thousand

*John Trumbull's painting of the signing of the Declaration of Independence
**No longer in circulation

• *The Great Seal of the United States.* The Seal is on the reverse side of our notes. It took more than six years before this seal was adopted. In 1776, the Continental Congress appointed Benjamin Franklin, Thomas Jefferson, and John Adams to come up with a seal for the country. This committee and others labored over designs for six years. A final committee asked William Barton,

GOOD-LOOKING MONEY

Keeping money looking good is the job of the Federal Reserve Banks and the U.S. Treasury Department. The average lifetime for a dollar bill ($1) is only 15 to 18 months. Then it becomes too dirty or ragged to use. Larger denominations last a little longer because they are used less frequently.

Each day, millions of dollars of deposits made in Federal Reserve Banks by depository institutions are carefully examined. Worn or mutilated notes are destroyed. Only Federal Reserve Banks and their branches, and in certain cases, the Treasury, are allowed to destroy money. At the New York Reserve Bank, for instance, about $35 million in paper currency is destroyed each day under strictly controlled procedures.

Up until very recently, all currency was destroyed by burning notes in an incinerator where temperatures up to 1,800 degrees reduced the currency to a white ash that looked like talcum powder. Now, most Federal Reserve

Banks put unfit currency through a sorter where stainless steel blades cut the notes lengthwise into 1/8 inch strips. The strips go by vacuum tube to a disposal area where shreds from each sorter are mixed together. The strips are then compressed by machine into 400-pound bales. One bale made up of shredded $20 bills contains approximately $4.5 million.

A private contractor picks up the bales and discards them at pre-designated landfills, or sells them to businesses. They are used by:

• oil well contractors to fill in the space previously occupied by rock and dirt in the well;

• companies which burn it for use in generators.

Destroyed money cannot be used for:

• printing paper of any kind (in order to avoid counterfeiting)

• containers holding foods or liquids consumed by people (because the ink contains toxic materials).

Bails of used money.

an authority on **heraldry**, to create a design. He submitted two, one of which was simplified by Charles Thompson, Secretary of the Congress. Congress adopted this design in 1782.

The face of the Seal on the right hand side of a $1 bill shows the American bald eagle with its wings and claws stretched out. Above its head is a "glory," or burst of light, containing 13 stars. The eagle's breast is covered by a shield with 13 stripes.

The right claw holds an olive branch with 13 leaves, representing peace; and the left holds a bundle of 13 arrows, symbolizing war. The eagle's head is turned toward the olive branch, symbolizing a desire for peace over war. The use of 13 so many times, of course, represents the original 13 colonies.

The top of the shield is said to represent Congress; the head of the eagle, the Executive Branch; and the nine tail feathers, the Judiciary. The Latin motto, on a ribbon held in the bird's beak, "E Pluribus Unum," means "Out of Many, One." Note that the Latin phrase has 13 letters!

The back of the seal has an unfinished pyramid, symbolizing material strength, a foundation for future growth and a goal of perfection. Above the pyramid is "glory" with an eye inside a triangle, representing the eternal eye of God. Note that the spiritual symbol is placed above the symbol for material wealth. At the top and around the edge are 13 letters in Latin, "Annuit Coeptis," meaning "He Has Favored our Undertakings." The base of the pyramid has the numerals for 1776. Below that is the motto "Novu Ordo Seclorum," or "A New Order of the Ages."

• *In God We Trust.* All denominations of both paper money and coin being issued bear this motto. It first appeared on a coin in 1864 because of the highly religious sentiment during the Civil War. Salmon P. Chase, then the Secretary of the Treasury, authorized its use after many citizens urged that some recognition of the Deity be included on our coins, as it was in other countries.

• *What Our Coins Look Like.* Our coins have changed many times since 1792 when the Coinage Act adopted the dollar as our standard monetary unit and established the U.S. Mint in Philadelphia. The Mint, which produces our coins, is a division of the Treasury Department. Designs for our coins are selected by the Director of the Mint, with the approval of the Secretary of the Treasury. Approval from Congress is not necessary, although Congress may prescribe a coin design. Once a design is used, it cannot be changed for 25 years, unless Congress votes otherwise.

In addition to the Philadelphia Mint, which has been striking coins since it was authorized in 1792,

THE GROWTH OF ECONOMICS

Gresham's Law. In the sixteenth century, Queen Elizabeth's Master of the Mint, Thomas Gresham, devised the theory that when two metals, such as gold and silver, are circulated as money, the cheaper money in the long run becomes the dominant coin in use. The other, more expensive metal is hoarded, sold to other countries, or melted down.

This principle, that "cheap money drives expensive money from circulation," is known as Gresham's Law. Some say "bad money drives out good."

Mercantilism. The theory of mercantilism was popular in seventeenth century Europe. Mercantilists said that countries could be powerful and wealthy if they accumulated gold and silver, and if they sold more merchandise than they bought. This led to establishing colonies and taking raw goods and precious metals from the colonies and in turn selling them goods.

Adam Smith. In 1776, a Scottish professor of philosophy, Adam Smith, published a book entitled *The Wealth of Nations* in which he argued that the source of national power and wealth was not gold and silver as the mercantilists believed, but rather the production of goods. Smith's book became the foundation for a new type of social science called "economics." His writings and those of followers were instrumental in getting Europe to improve production and develop inter-dependent trade.

Irving Fisher. In 1911, this American mathematician and economist proved that doubling the nation's money supply would double the prices of things. He said that economic booms and busts were the result of too much or too little money. Fisher's studies led to a new approach to economics called "econometrics."

Milton Friedman. In the 1950s, this American economist supported Fisher's theories and even added to them. Friedman said changes in the amount of money in circulation influence the economy's direction, the rate of production, and how much we spend. In order to have a stable economy, according to Friedman, the money supply must increase steadily in proportion to production. This theory, called "monetarism," has influenced the way the Federal Reserve controls our money supply.

YOU'VE COME A LONG WAY

The Susan B. Anthony one dollar coin is the first one commemorating a "real" woman on a U.S. coin. (The mythical female known as "Liberty" has appeared on various types of our money.) Susan B. Anthony, best known for her efforts to get women the right to vote, appears on one side of the coin. The passage of the 19th amendment to the Constitution, granting women that right, came four-teen years after her death. The other side shows an eagle landing on the moon, symbolic of the tenth anniversary of the landing of the Apollo 11 spacecraft, "The Eagle," on the moon on July 20, 1969.

The only U.S. paper currency ever to have the portrait of a woman was the 1886 one dollar Silver Certificate. The woman was Martha Washington.

Susan B. Anthony

there are two branch mints in operation today—the Denver Mint and the San Francisco Mint.

The San Francisco Mint, known as the "Granite Lady," is famous because it miraculously survived the devastating San Francisco Earthquake and subsequent fire of 1906 that destroyed much of that city. In fact, the Granite Lady actually saved the city from total economic collapse because it was the only financial institution able to handle money and so it became the temporary treasury for relief funds.

Although the building was surrounded by flames, Army soldiers and many heroic employees of the Mint fought the fire for seven hours using one inch hoses.

Today, the Granite Lady is a Mint Museum, open to the public.

The Gold Standard

The United States was officially on a gold standard from 1900 to 1933. Until that time, all our money was redeemable in gold at the U.S. Treasury. Being on a gold standard meant an official price for gold was established and that there was unlimited convertibility between currency and gold at that price. This meant that the money supply was limited by the amount of gold in the Treasury. When we were on the gold standard, every dollar bill bore the following inscription:

"The United States of America Will Pay to the Bearer on Demand One Dollar in Gold."

Then, almost overnight, owning gold was declared illegal by an Executive Order issued by President Franklin D. Roosevelt on April 5, 1933. The inscription was changed to read:

"The United States of America Will Pay to the Bearer on Demand One Dollar in Lawful Money."

Bankers are just like anyone else except richer.

—Ogden Nash, 1953

In 1947, A.F. Davis of Cleveland, Ohio, decided to test this out. He sent a $10 bill to the Treasury, requesting the lawful money in exchange. He received two $5 bills in the mail.

In 1964, the inscription was removed from our currency. Today all that is said is: "This note is legal tender for all debts, public and private," and in much larger print: "In God We Trust."

With the gold standard, the public and not the Federal Reserve determines the money supply. The public does so by hoarding gold and reducing the supply, which in turn can intensify a recession. When this happens, or even if people think it will, they buy as much gold as possible before the price rises and then they sell it back to the government after the price has moved up. This is exactly why the gold standard was abandoned in 1933.

THE MEDICI BANKERS

The Medici of Florence were the world's leading bankers and merchant princes from 1400 to the 1740s. For nearly three and a half centuries, in fact, their bank was the most advanced financial institution of its time. The Medici rose from being modest merchants to controlling much of Europe's money supply. By using their vast land holdings and close connections with the wealthy Popes of their day, they sustained a life style like that of great royalty. Two factors led to their importance: the expansion of economic trade during the Crusades and the huge sums of money collected by the Popes, which Medici and other Italian banking families then handled. Ironically, their famous emblem—red balls on a gold background—was originally a pawnbroker's sign.

Cosimo de' Medici (1389–1464) was the first in the family to become the undisputed ruler of Florence. In 1429 he inherited the Medici bank, which was then the largest business in Europe. Cosimo possessed a unique combination of business skills and scholarly interests, which enabled him to rule by wealth rather than by force and to use his money and influence for social improvements. He expanded the family's holdings so that the Medici bank had branches in Rome, Milan, Geneva, Bruges, Pisa, London, and Avignon. Although Cosimo and his family owned the largest shares in these branches, he permitted local managers and investors to share in the banks' prof-

Lorenzo de' Medici

its, an innovative idea at the time.

Cosimo and his successors were not only leaders in banking techniques, but in architecture as well. They pioneered the idea that banks should have impressive, palatial surroundings, a concept still at work today. Cosimo also encouraged some of the world's greatest artists— Ghiberti, Brunelleschi, Donatello, Fra Angelico, Lippi and Uccello—and in 1444, he founded what was probably the first major public library in Europe, devoting his own time and money to purchasing rare manuscripts and works of ancient authors.

Cosimo's grandson, Lorenzo de' Medici, "The Magnificent" (1449–1492), became a benefactor of the arts on an even grander scale. He is perhaps best known as the first patron of Michelangelo and a major buyer of works by Verrocchio and Botticelli. Lorenzo was also a poet—some scholars say the greatest Italian poet of the 15th century. He organized elaborate festivals for religious and state holidays and supported a glamorous court of great thinkers. Although this Renaissance prince made Florence the artistic and intellectual capital of Europe, the Medici bank could not sustain his adventures. After his death in 1492, it eventually lost its position to rival Italian and German banks. The Medici continued, however, to play a role in Italian events for some time, producing politicians, patrons of the arts, and the two Medici popes—Leo X and Clement VII.

Savings accounts help people of any age earn interest on their deposits.

3

SAVINGS ACCOUNTS

When you receive money for your birthday or from an after-school job, you face an immediate and important financial decision: whether to spend it on something you've always wanted, such as a tape or a sweater, or to save it and spend it later—a day later, a month later, or even years later. The best place to keep your money is in a **savings account** at a bank. Of course, you could keep it in your piggy bank or savings jar at home, but if you do, you miss out on one of the easiest ways to make money—by earning interest. That's because if you deposit your money, even a very small amount, in a savings account, it will earn interest. (Interest is the amount of money a bank pays you for leaving your money in an account. It is expressed as a percentage, such as 5 percent.)

Savings account: A bank account in which the depositor's money earns interest. The money is available at any time.

Although banks can pay whatever rate they wish on savings accounts, most pay about 5 1/2 percent. Although other types of accounts may pay higher rates, this is the best place to start, especially if you only have a small amount of money with which to open the account.

Opening a Savings Account

When you open your first bank account, you will need your Social Security number and perhaps one other form of identification. If you are not old enough for a driver's license or a learner's permit, most banks will accept a library card or school ID showing your address. Some banks, however, may ask a parent to sign the application as well. The Social Security number is required because any interest you earn will be reported to the Internal Revenue Service. Check with your parents or their accountant to see if you will owe taxes on money earned in your savings account. You can also get a free booklet explaining taxes for kids, sometimes called the Kiddie Tax, by calling the IRS at 800-424-FORM. Ask for brochure #922, "Tax Rules for Children and Dependents."

Passbook and Statement Accounts

There are two basic types of savings accounts: a passbook account and a monthly statement account. In order to open either type of account, call or visit your bank and ask about their **minimum deposit** requirement. In a small town bank it may be as little as $5, while a larger bank may require $100 or more. Your bank may give savers a small book, like a thin paperback booklet, in which all **deposits**, **withdrawals**, and interest payments are recorded. However, many banks have done away with the actual book and instead record transactions only in

I've got all the money I'll ever need if I die by four o'clock.

—Henny Youngman

Minimum deposit: The smallest dollar amount required to open an account.

Deposit: The act of putting money into a bank account; the opposite of withdrawal. A person who deposits money in a bank is called a depositor.

Withdrawal: Taking money out of a bank account.

the bank's computer. (Transactions in a passbook account are also entered in the bank's computers.) This type of account, the statement savings account, provides savers with a **monthly statement** of all transactions. These statements are mailed to each saver. If your account is inactive, meaning you have not made a deposit or a withdrawal during a certain time period, some banks charge a small monthly fee and/or send statements only quarterly to reduce their expenses.

The advantage of a statement savings account is that you do not have to worry about losing your savings book, which is time-consuming to replace.

Most banks have either a passbook savings or a statement-type account and do not give you a choice. Some, however, have both and may pay a slightly higher interest rate to encourage customers to use a statement account because it is less expensive for them to operate.

The money you deposit in a savings account is always immediately available to you. Bankers call this instant availability of money **liquidity**. Usually there is no limit on the amount you can put in or take out, nor on how frequently you can make these transactions. You can make **periodic** deposits until you have enough money to transfer to another type of account that pays a higher rate of interest. We will explain those accounts on pages 93–97.

To deposit money, you must fill out a "deposit form" or slip. Present that form with your savings book or statement to the bank **teller**.

To withdraw money from your savings account, fill out a withdrawal slip, such as the one shown below, and present it to the teller along with your passbook or savings statement. Banks reserve the right to refuse withdrawal requests if customers do not present appropriate identification.

Monthly statement: A summary of an account's activity during a thirty-day period. It shows deposits, withdrawals, and interest earned. A monthly statement for a credit card lists purchases, the date of purchase, price, amount due, and interest rate charged if the amount due is not paid in full.

Liquidity: Refers to the assets that can easily and quickly be converted into cash, without substantial loss, such as savings and checking account deposits.

Periodic: Payments made over time, usually but not necessarily at fixed intervals, such as the first of every month.

Teller: The bank employee who accepts deposits and gives out withdrawals to customers.

Your monthly statement, if you have a statement type account, will list these items:

• Your balance on the date the statement was prepared

• An itemized listing by date of deposits

• An itemized listing by date of interest payments

• The total amount of interest credited to your account

• A summary section indicating all deposits, interest earned, and withdrawals made to the account during the period covered by the statement.

If you have a passbook instead of a statement account, you can have it brought up-to-date by mailing or bringing it into the bank. Although most banks allow customers to make deposits by mail, never send cash through the mail.

Compound: Interest paid upon the principal plus the interest already earned.

QUESTIONS TO ASK YOUR BANKER

These are the questions you want to ask your banker when you open your first savings account:

• What is the minimum deposit?

• What is the interest rate?

• Is there a minimum balance that must be maintained in order to earn that rate of interest?

• If my account falls below the minimum balance, is there a fee? If so, how much?

• How is the interest **compounded**? Quarterly, monthly, daily, or continuously? (The more frequently, the better for you. See table on page 47.)

• How often can I put money in? Take it out?

• Is there a monthly service fee?

• What if I don't make deposits or withdrawals for a long time? Will there be a fee? (Some banks charge a fee for inactive accounts.)

Holiday Savings Clubs

Your bank may offer a Vacation, Christmas, or Hanukkah Savings Club. These special purpose savings accounts help people save money. There is one drawback, however: many pay no interest or very low rates. Nevertheless, the accounts encourage people to make weekly or biweekly deposits by turning in a coupon from their coupon booklet each time they put money in the bank. These coupons may be pre-stamped with a deposit due date, such as the first or fifteenth of each month.

Bank holiday clubs let people save for special occasions.

Some banks do not have coupon books, but instead automatically transfer money from your checking account to your holiday club account every week or month. You determine the amount and how often you want deposits transferred.

If you save this amount each week for 50 weeks . . . you will have:

$10	$ 500
$20	$ 1,000
$50	$ 2,500

(plus whatever interest the bank pays)

Trust Accounts

Savings accounts are often opened by an adult "in trust for" someone else, usually a **minor**. This person is called the **beneficiary** because he is the one that will eventually benefit from the money in the account. The account owner, the person who puts the money in the account, controls the account. That means he or she is the only one who can make withdrawals. When that person dies, the money goes to the beneficiary. The account owner can change the beneficiary at any time by signing a change of beneficiary form at the bank. This type of account is sometimes called a "Totten Trust."

Minor: Someone who is not legally an adult; the legal age is usually 21 or 18 depending upon the state in which one lives.

Beneficiary: The person designated to receive the income from an account held in trust for that person.

Uniform Gift to Minors Account

Also known as a custodial account, this account is like a trust account, in that it is a way of transferring money to someone else. It is less flexible than the trust account because once a custodial account is set up, the money in the account legally belongs to the person named, frequently a child. In other words, the gift of money to a minor is **irrevocable**. The custodian or person who opens and funds the account can determine how the money is invested but he or she cannot withdraw the funds except to use for the child's benefit. When the child reaches legal age (twenty-one or eighteen depending upon the state) full control of the money in the account *must* be turned over to the minor by the custodian.

Irrevocable: Cannot be reversed or changed; refers to an irrevocable trust in which the grantor gives up all rights to end or change the arrangement.

How Money Grows: The Magic of Interest Rates and Compounding

One advantage of putting money you don't need right away in a savings account is that it's out of the way and you won't be tempted to spend it as you would if it were in your pocket. But another great plus is that your money earns interest. This interest is added to the **principal** on a regular basis. On top of that, the interest is compounded. At the end of each interest period, interest is calculated on the total amount—the principal and the interest already in the account. If you left your money at home you would lose out on this very simple way to earn money on money.

Principal: The amount invested as distinguished from interest or profits.

You can see how beneficial compounding is by using the "Rule of 72." (See box, next page.)

• *Types of Yields.* Compounding, or earning interest on interest plus principal, is what makes the "effective annual **yield**." Bank advertisements for savings account, and other types of accounts, too, often give two figures: the annual interest rate and

Yield: Rate of return earned on a deposit or security.

THE RULE OF 72

Here's an easy way to determine how fast your savings will grow at different interest rates. The rule of 72 shows how long it takes to double your money if interest is compounded annually.

Divide 72 by the interest rate the bank is paying. For example, if the rate is 5 percent, it will take fourteen years and four months for your money to double. But if the rate is 8 percent, it will take only nine years.

Rate of Interest	Years Until Money Is Doubled
5%	14.4 years
6	12.0
7	10.2
8	9.0
9	8.0
10	7.2

the effective yield, which is the higher number. The difference between these two figures is due to the frequency with which interest is credited to your balance and therefore the greater the principal amount on which interest is paid. The more frequently interest is compounded, the faster your money will grow. Interest can be compounded daily, weekly, monthly, quarterly, or annually. For instance, a 5 percent interest rate has an affective yield of 5 percent if the interest is credited annually. The effective yield, however, will be 5.094 percent if it is credited quarterly and 5.116 percent if interest is credited monthly. Although these amounts seem insignificant on small deposits, the difference can be important when one has large amounts in a savings account.

For many years, interest rates on savings accounts were regulated by law, but today banks can pay whatever rates they wish. Some banks, to attract new customers, will pay higher rates than others, even though they are in the same town or city. In fact, banks right across the street from one another may have different rates. So, take time to find the best rate possible. It's not just a matter of which bank advertises the highest rate. You need to look closely at a number of factors:

• Service fees can reduce your yield.

• The more frequently interest is compounded, the more money you will earn in your account.

• The best deal is when a bank calculates interest from day of deposit to day of withdrawal. Otherwise, if you take out money in the middle of a **quarter**, you will lose interest for the entire quarter.

Quarter: A three-month period of the year. The first quarter consists of January, February, and March.

• You'll earn more money if interest is calculated on the entire amount in your savings account. Some banks calculate on the lowest balance in the account during the interest period.

The bank's printed literature should describe how interest is calculated, but if it does not, or if it is not clear, be certain to ask a bank official to explain it to you. Your money should start to earn interest on the day it is deposited, provided you deposit it by 3 P.M. on a **business day**. If you deposit your money after 3 P.M. it will start to earn interest as of the next business day.

Business day: All days except Saturday, Sunday and federal holidays; the business day for banks ends at 3 p.m.

It is also important to know the balance on which interest is computed. Some pay interest on the lowest balance, which is to be avoided if possible. For example, if your balance since September 1 has been $1,500, but you withdraw $1,000 on September 29, your interest for September will be based on only the $500.

You now know how savings accounts work and how money in such an account earns even more money through the compounding of interest. Now let's find out how you can move money about. In the next two chapters we will examine the various bank services that help us pay bills.

LOST MONEY

Every year more than $1 billion in property goes unclaimed. Part of it could belong to someone you or your family knows. The government estimates that one in ten people is owed some type of unclaimed property, including bank accounts, utility deposits, insurance policies, stocks, bonds, and even payroll or pension checks.

How does this happen? Usually it's because people move and neglect to leave their new address, or their recorded address is incorrect.

Laws defining when property is considered abandoned vary from state to state and by type of asset, but most statutes require that property be turned over to the state treasurer after being unclaimed for five to seven years. Many states try to find the rightful owners by publishing a list of names in local newspapers. Some cross-check names with state tax and motor vehicle records. Even so, they only find thirty to fifty percent of the rightful owners. Although the law says abandoned property can be claimed "in perpetuity" forever, the majority of states actually use the unclaimed money, maintaining a small reserve for any positive claims. The largest source of abandoned property is dormant bank accounts.

Where Is It and Is It Yours?
Here's where you may find money that belongs to someone in your family:
• *Unclaimed Bank Accounts*: Contact the Office of the State Treasurer, Department of Revenue, or State Comptroller, Unclaimed Property Division, for the state you now live in and where you previously lived. The appropriate address and number is listed in the Government Section of the telephone book.

Most states accept phone inquiries, but some require written requests.
• *Social Security*: Over $600 million in Social Security payments are still uncashed. Check with your local Social Security office.
• *U.S. Savings Bonds and Treasury Issues*: Many people apparently forget to cash in their savings bonds. Contact the Savings Bond Office, Correspondence & Claims Branch, 200 Third Street, Parkersburg, West Virginia 26106-1328. Give the original owner's name and address, issue date, denomination, and serial number, if possible.
• *Veterans Administration*: This agency, which issues pension benefits to war vets, does not keep track of undelivered or uncashed checks. Veterans should call their nearest VA office and give their supply name, years in the service, birth date, and Social Security number.
• *Internal Revenue Service*: Recently a Freedom of Information request filed by the National Taxpayers Union found $25.7 million in unclaimed tax refund checks issued over a three-year period. The average check was $425. Anyone who thinks they're missing a refund check should fill out the Taxpayer's Statement Regarding Fund, Form 3911, available at their district IRS office.
• *Federal Housing Administration*: Unclaimed mortgage insurance premiums are easy to forget about. Contact: Department of Finance & Accounting, Distributive Shares Branch, Washington, D.C. 20410-3411, or call their hotline at 202-755-5616. You'll need the property's address, name of lender, and the mortgage FHA case number.

Checking accounts need to be balanced regularly.

4

CHECKING ACCOUNTS

At some point you will need to give money to someone else—to pay bills, to buy something, to pay back a loan. If small amounts are involved and if this occurs only now and then, you can use cash. But as soon as you need to pay out larger sums of money or even small sums on a regular basis, it's time to open a checking account. Checking accounts are one of those financial necessities of life.

The purpose of a checking account is to safely transfer money and to have a record of that transfer. Factories and businesses pay workers by checks. The government makes tax refunds by check. People pay their grocery and telephone bills by check . . . nearly every conceivable item has been paid for at one time or another by check. According to the Federal Reserve, some 40 billion checks are written every year. Sooner or later, you will be one of those people writing checks. To do so, you must open a checking account.

There are two basic types of accounts to choose from, although individual banks often add their own special features. Your local banker can explain such details about his or her bank, but here are the usual features of the two types:

Regular Checking Accounts

These are also called noninterest bearing accounts. As the name implies, you do not earn interest on the money in your account, as you would with a savings account. In most cases you must pay the bank to provide this checking service, either a monthly fee or a per-check fee, although some banks offer free checking. Usually, but certainly not in every case, regular checking accounts are the cheapest, especially for those who keep small balances or who write only a few checks per month.

An example of one bank's different fees for regular checking is shown on page 56. Monthly maintenance charges can be offset by deposit balances.

Checking Accounts That Pay Interest

These pay the depositor interest on the balance kept in the account. NOW Accounts (which stand for negotiable order of withdrawal) is the overall or **generic name** for these accounts but each bank may use its own **brand name**, such as "High Interest Checking." Each bank has different balance requirements and pays different rates of interest on these balances.

Most banks also offer **overdraft checking** for both interest and noninterest bearing accounts. This is a permanent line of credit that prevents you from

Generic name: General name for an entire group; a name that is commonly available and not protected by a trademark.

Brand name: A name that is protected by trademark and cannot be used by anyone else.

Overdraft checking: An account in which checks written against insufficient funds are covered by the bank. The bank loans the owner of the checking account money to cover the check.

RECONCILING YOUR CHECKING ACCOUNT

In Your Checkbook
1. List your checkbook balance: $_____
2. Subtract the service charge: $_____
3. Your balance: $_____

On The Bank Statement
1. List your bank statement balance: $_____
2. List checks outstanding:

    Check number   Amount

    _____ $_____

    _____ $_____

    _____ $_____

    _____ $_____

3. Subtract checks outstanding: $_____
4. Subtotal: $_____
5. Add any deposits not credited $_____
   on your statement:
6. Your checkbook balance should be: $_____

bouncing a check. The bank will automatically cover or pay your check, even if you don't have money in the account. However, you will have to pay back the loan plus interest.

Bounced check: One that is not paid because of insufficient funds in the account.

Selecting the Right Type of Checking Account

It seems logical, doesn't it, that an account that pays interest is better than one that does not? Unfortunately, that isn't always the case. Interest-bearing checking accounts frequently have fairly high monthly fees or other charges. For example, if you dip below a certain dollar amount, the bank may stop paying interest, reduce the interest rate, or level a fee. If these fees and other charges add up to more than the amount of interest the account earns, as is often the case if there's a low balance in the account, then an account that pays interest may not be the best choice.

Most people choose a bank for convenience, because it is near their home, office, or school. Convenience is an important consideration, but you should also find out: 1) how much the bank charges for checks, and if it is a per-check charge or a flat monthly fee; 2) if you need to maintain a minimum balance to earn interest or to avoid fees; and 3) if interest is paid, the rate and whether it is paid on the entire balance or only if you maintain a certain balance. *Note:* Some banks have tiered rates, which means depositors get a higher rate for keeping larger amounts in the account. For example, if

Sample Check

Front

Jane Doe **1 Main Street** **Anwhere, State ZIP**	*March 3,* 19 *91*

Pay to the
Order of *John Q. Public* $ *50.43*

Fifty and 43/100—————————————————————— dollars

Bank   **Last National Savings**
City, State
123456789 0000000 0000 00 0000   *Jane Doe*

Account number   **Signature**

Back

Area 1		Area 2		Area 3
1"				3"
John Q. Public		Reserved for bank into which check is first deposited		

you keep less than $500 in the account, you may get 5 percent interest on the entire balance, but if you keep $500 to $2,000 you will earn 5 1/2 percent or 6 percent on the entire balance. On amounts over $2,000, it may be 6 1/4 percent.

Here are the terms you need to know to make a smart checking account decision:

• *Flat fee.* The bank charges a flat fee no matter how much money you keep in your account or how many checks you write.

• *Minimum balance.* The bank charges a monthly fee, based on minimum balance requirements. If you keep a certain average daily balance for a month, you may not have to pay any fee that month. If you drop below that minimum, you trigger a fee.

• *Tiered pricing.* Fees are calculated on various dollar balances. See examples above.

• *Per-check fee.* This fee is sometimes imposed in addition to a monthly fee or instead of it. When per-check costs are charged, monthly fees tend to be lower.

• *Free checking.* This is increasingly rare, but some small town banks still offer free checking.

Money can't buy friends, but you can get a better class of enemy.

—Spike Mulligan

How to Write a Check

After you open your account, the bank will give you a checkbook and deposit slips. You can have your name and address printed on both if you like. Or you can have them left blank. Most people do not have their telephone number on their checks for safety reasons. Your account number will also appear on each check and deposit slip.

Your checkbook has two sections: one consists of the actual checks and the other the check stub or register. The check stub shows the number of the check and has lines to fill in for the date that you

BANK FEES

Monthly Average Checking Balance	Monthly Maintenance Charge
$1,500 or more	none
$750 - $1,500 and $5,000 in other bank accounts in the same bank	none
Under $750 and $5,000 in other bank accounts in the same bank	$7
Under $1,500 and less than $5,000 in other accounts in the same bank	$15

write the check; the person, organization, or company you're paying; and the dollar amount of the check. (See example on page 54.) Fill out the check stub before writing the check. After you've filled in the amount of the check, subtract it from the previous balance. Then follow these six steps:

1) *Fill in the check number.* Most checks are prenumbered when they are printed, although you can order unnumbered checks if you prefer. If you do, number the checks **consecutively**.

Consecutively: Numbered in regular sequence, such as 1, 2, 3, etc.

2) *Date the check.* Write in the actual date you are writing the check. It is not a good idea to date a check with a future date because the bank cannot pay it if it is presented there for payment before that date. (Dating a check ahead of time is called "postdating.")

3) *Write in the payee's name.* The payee is the person, business, or organization you are paying. You are the payor. Write the name on the line labeled: "Pay to the order of." If you are writing a

check to get cash for yourself, then fill in your own name or write the word "cash" on the payee line.

4) *Fill in the figures.* Write the amount you are paying very close to the pre-printed dollar sign. Write clearly.

5) *Fill in the dollar and cents amount in words.* This, of course, is the same amount that you filled in in figures. Begin writing at the far left end of the line and spell out the dollar amount, "Twelve," for example. Then write the number of cents as a fraction over the number 100: 98/100 means you are paying $12.98. Use a wavy line to fill out the leftover space.

6) *Sign the check.* Use the same signature every time. It should match the one you used when you opened your account. If that read: Abigail T. Campbell, then always use that and never simply Abigail Campbell or A.T. Campbell.

How to Endorse a Check

When you receive a check that you wish to deposit, either into your checking or savings account, you must first **endorse** it, that is, sign your name on the back side in the upper quarter of the check. Many checks have a line to write on. If not, write as closely as possible to the top. (See diagram.) Avoid writing in area #2, which is the space used by the bank in which the check is first deposited. If for some reason your endorsement does not fit into area #1, perhaps because you need to add an address, telephone number, or driver's license number, you can use the space in area #3. Never use area #2.

Endorsement: One's signature by which the endorser transfers the money represented by a check to someone else.

Endorse or write your name *exactly* as it appears on the face or front of the check. Even if your name is misspelled on the face, or given incorrectly, endorse it on the back in the same way. Then, write your correct signature below it. For example: If the check is incorrectly made out to Abigalle Campbell, endorse it that way and underneath write Abigail T. Campbell, your official name. The safest way to endorse a check is to write "for deposit only in" and fill in the name of the bank.

Then write your name and account number. That way, no one can double endorse the check and you know it will be deposited into your account. A double endorsed check is made payable to someone else and then endorsed to you by that person.

If you do not want to put it in your account, but instead wish to transfer this money to someone else, you may write, "Pay to the order of" and the person's name, followed by your own signature.

Keep these points in mind:

• Always use a pen, typewriter, or check-writing machine. Never use a pencil to make out or endorse a check. Banks prefer blue or black ink.

• If you make a mistake when making out a check, tear it up. Don't cross it out and try to correct it. Then write "void" next to that number in your record or stub book.

• Never lend out your checks or borrow someone else's. The bank's computer can read the original code, even if it's inked out, and will automatically put it into that account.

• If you deposit checks by mail, be certain to endorse them on the back with the words "for deposit only" and add your account number. Never send cash through the mail. If for some reason it is absolutely necessary, send it by registered mail.

Stop payment: A request by a depositor to the bank to refuse to pay a certain check when it is returned to the bank.

• If you want to **stop payment** on a check, call your bank immediately. Stop payments are necessary when you don't have enough money in your checking account to cover the check, because a check has been lost or stolen, or because the person or company did not deliver the items or service you're paying for. Give the bank the date of the check, the amount, and the name of the payee. The bank will charge for each stop payment you make.

• If you lose your checkbook, notify the bank at once. You will probably be asked to close the account and put a stop payment on all outstanding checks.

Checks let people buy merchandise without using cash.

Knowing When Your Money Is Available

If you deposit a check into your account that is *drawn* or made out on another bank, the money is not collected until it has been accepted by the bank on which it was drawn. In other words, when you deposit a check, your bank only has a piece of paper until it collects the funds from the other bank. The time it takes to collect this money, or for the check "to clear," varies depending on the type of check you deposit and the location of the bank. As of September 1, 1990, the money from **local checks** must generally be cleared or available on the second business day after your deposit. Nonlocal checks must generally be cleared by the fifth business day after your deposit.

Local check: A check that is deposited in an institution in the same Federal Reserve check-processing region as the paying bank.

Certain types of checks will be cleared on the business day following the business day of deposit. These include cash and traveler's checks, deposits made electronically, such as Social Security payments and wire transfers, U.S. Treasury checks, Federal Reserve checks, U.S. Postal Money Orders, state and local government checks, cashier's checks, teller's checks, and certified checks.

Checks made out for $49.99 or less are available on the following business day. The first $100 of a larger deposit is also available the following business day.

Deposits made at an automated teller machine (ATM) are handled differently. Check with your bank.

The new rules for check clearing don't necessarily apply to certain types of deposits. Banks may delay clearing on:

• *New deposits.* For the first 30 days your new account is open, special check clearing rules apply. Ask your banker.

• *Overdrawn accounts.* If your account has frequently been overdrawn, the bank may delay the availability of funds.

• *Double-endorsed checks.* A check that is not made payable directly to you can be held longer before clearing.

• *Unpaid checks.* A check that was deposited once, returned unpaid and deposited again.

• *Foreign checks.* Checks drawn on banks outside the United States generally do not clear until the funds have been received by your bank from the bank on which the check is drawn.

How to Balance Your Checkbook

Once a month, the bank will send you a statement of your account. (See example.) This lists all the deposits made and all the checks received and paid by the bank during a certain time period, usually 30 days. It is very important that your checkbook and the bank statement agree or match. The last number on your statement should be the same as the number in your checkbook for the same date. If they do not match, it could be because:

• Some checks you wrote have not yet been returned to your bank for payment,

• or some of your deposits may not have been credited to your account yet,

• or there is a mistake in addition or subtraction, made by you or the bank. (Banks do make errors!)

Take time to reconcile your statement with your checkbook when you receive your monthly statement. It's quite simple:

1) First look at all the returned checks. Make certain they are yours and put them in order, by check number or by date.

2) Pencil a checkmark on each check and next to each entry on the statement when they match.

Balancing a Checkbook

(1) Enter in your checkbook any interest earned on your account as it appears on the front of the statement.

(2) Verify that checks are charged correctly on statement for amount drawn.

(3) Be sure that the service charge (if any) or other withdrawals shown on this statement have been deducted from your checkbook balance.

(4) Verify that all deposits are for the same amount as on your records.

(5) Check off on the stubs of your checkbook each of the checks paid by the bank.

(6) Make a list of the numbers and amounts of those checks still outstanding in the space provided below.

(7)	Enter Final Balance as per Statement		
(8)	**ADD** Any Deposits Not Credited		
(9)	Total		
(10)	**SUBTRACT** Checks Outstanding		
(11)	**BALANCE** Should Agree with Checkbook		

3) Then match the returned checks with the entries in your checkbook. They too should match. If there is a stub for a check which has not been returned to you, then that check has not yet cleared. It should be listed as "outstanding."

4) Subtract all outstanding checks from the balance shown on your statement.

5) Check off the deposits shown on the statement against those in your checkbook. Add any deposits made after the closing date on the statement to the end balance.

6) The balance on your statement (plus deposits minus any outstanding checks) should match the current balance in your checkbook. Be certain you have included any service charges.

If the balances disagree. If the balance in your checkbook and the bank statement do not agree, then you must look for an error. Perhaps you entered an incorrect amount or made a mathematical error. Maybe you forgot to enter a check or a deposit. It's also possible that the bank made an

error. If so, notify them immediately.

You should subtract each check total from your balance each time you write one and not wait until you receive the monthly statement. Knowing how much money you have left in your account prevents you from writing bounced checks. Banks charge a hefty service fee for bounced checks and it's embarrassing. You must call the person you wrote the check to and explain that there wasn't enough money in your account to cover the check. Then you'll have to write a new check. To help avoid this problem, many banks offer a line of credit, or pre-approved loan amount, that automatically covers your check if the account does not have enough money. If you use this line of credit, the bank will charge interest, but if you pay back the loan at once, it may be less expensive than paying the bounced check penalty. And it certainly saves you the nuisance and embarrassment of calling the person or business you sent the check to and asking them not to cash it because of insufficient funds.

ALL-KIDS BANKS

Banking is not just for adults. Two banks in this country, The Young Americans Bank in Denver and The First Children's Bank in New York, are designed for kids only. Both offer checking and savings accounts as well as other special features. Because parents or guardians are legally responsible for their children's financial matters until they are eighteen or twenty-one, they must sign the documents allowing kids to open accounts.

•In New York

Kids can have special accounts at The First Children's Bank, located in the famous toy store, F.A.O. Schwarz. Opened in 1988, its purpose is to teach children how a bank works and parents how they can help meet their childrens' future financial needs. The idea for the bank came from a four-year-old girl who asked her mother why there was a bank for adults but not for children. Customers must be under the age of eighteen to open an account, or under twenty-one for "The College CD." The minimum age for a checking account is six. Checking and savings accounts can be opened for $50. Deposits to checking or savings must be $1 or more. Cash withdrawals are limited on weekends to $250. A student may make a deposit alone but needs an adult co-signer to make cash withdrawals. The checks are bright yellow and red

The First Children's Bank located in New York City.

and have two signature lines, one for the child and one for the adult. Checks can be used at F.A.O. Schwarz or anywhere else checks are accepted.

The bank's College CD is one of the best in the country. The minimum is $1,000. It has a floating interest rate so if rates move up so will the return, although if rates fall this is a disadvantage. Deposits of at least $250 can be added to the CD any time prior to the week before maturity, so savings can build quickly. The bank lets the investor select the length of the CD, which can be anywhere fron two to twenty years. A donation will be made by The First Chil dren's Bank to one of five children's charities in the name of the student when the CD's balance reaches $10,000, and for every $10,000 increment thereafter. The depositor selects a charity from the bank's list when the account is opened. The First Children's Bank also conducts financial seminars for parents and children.

Kids using a children's bank.

For more information, contact:

> The First Children's Bank
> c/o First New York Bank for
>   Business
> 111 East 57th Street
> New York, NY 10022

•In Denver

The idea for the Denver-based bank came to Bill Daniels, chairman of Daniels and Associates, Inc., a cable television company, when he read an article about students trying to get a loan for a Christmas project at their school. Realizing that young people want to participate in banking transactions, he committed his own money along with that of others to start the bank in 1987. As of January 1990, more than 11,000 savings accounts had been opened. Students who have a checking account may apply for an ATM card and use it at one of 12,000 machines through the CIRRUS network, withdrawing cash, making deposits, and transferring money between savings and checking. Kids can also deposit money for a fixed period in a CD and earn higher interest than on a savings account. Personal loans, business loans, and student educational loans are given. MasterCard is available to those age twelve and older who have written consent from their parents. There is a $100 credit limit and a $15 annual fee. Other services: traveler's checks, cashier's checks, gift certificates, and Savings Bonds. For more information, contact:

> Young Americans Bank
> 250 Steele Street
> Denver, CO 80206
> 303-321-2265

ATMs make deposits and withdrawals more convenient.

5

MOVING MONEY AROUND

I f you live near your bank, then you may enjoy doing all your transactions in person, perhaps at lunch time. But if you must be in school during banking hours or if you go away on vacation, you need to move your money around by other means. You have several choices ranging from the old-fashioned postal carrier to electronic transfer of funds.

Automated Teller Machines (ATMs)

The electronic age makes it possible to move money quickly and easily. Teller machines on street corners, in office buildings and supermarkets across the nation make depositing and withdrawing money possible 24 hours a day. ATMs now perform services previously available only from tellers.

ATM GUIDELINES

- Pick a PIN (personal identification number) you can remember so you won't have to write it down—your mother's birthday, perhaps. Do not carry it in your wallet or purse and do not share it with friends.
- Enter every ATM transaction in your checkbook. Keep the machine-issued transaction slips as well.
- If you deposit cash, check the transaction slip at the same time. If the machine made an error in recording the amount deposited, you should report it immediately.
- Check with your bank to see if it charges for ATM transactions. In large metropolitan areas, a card issued by one bank may be used in the ATM of another bank, but you will often be charged a fee.
- Be cautious when withdrawing cash from an ATM, especially at night or when the area is deserted.
- Visa and MasterCard can be used in many ATMs for cash advances. You may have to pay interest on these advances from the minute you receive the advance.

To use an ATM, you need a plastic card and a personal identification number, issued by the bank. The card and the code are required to make deposits, to transfer money from one account to another, and to make cash withdrawals. Each bank sets a limit on how much cash you can withdraw in any one day. If you're planning to get cash for a trip, be certain you know what your daily limit is.

Banking by Mail

If you're in school during banking hours, you can bank by mail, or use an ATM if there's one near your home or school. Ask your bank for its pre-printed, specially designed envelopes for making deposits by mail. Use these only for checks; never send cash in the mail. Fill in the required details and then, to further protect your envelope, tape it closed. *Note:* If in an emergency you must send cash via mail, get a money order from the post office or send the cash by registered mail.

Direct Deposits

As a student, you may receive payroll checks if you have a job. When you retire you'll get Social Security, or pension checks. You can have these kinds of checks automatically deposited into your account. It involves an electronic transfer of funds

Making a cash withdrawal.

from the employer, Social Security office, or other government agency to your bank account. Direct deposit saves you from having to make a trip to the bank. Your check is also treated as cash by the bank so your money is available immediately.

Until you are employed (or retired!) you can use a type of direct deposit. Ask to have money automatically transferred from your savings account to your checking account. This keeps some money earning interest as long as possible.

Banking at Home

In God we trust—
all others pay
cash.

—sign on an
Arkansas diner

A few of the nation's larger banks offer home banking services through the telephone and home computers. Customers dial the bank's computer and then get a display on their home TV screen or monitor to get their bank account balance and/or the amount of credit available on a credit card, such as Visa or MasterCard. Some systems enable subscribers to pay bills. Because these services are relatively new and fairly expensive, they are useful only to a limited number of people.

Paying Bills by Telephone

An increasing number of banks offer telephone bill-paying services. You must fill out an authorization form and give the bank a list of the people or businesses you need to pay on a regular basis. The bank will send you a numerical code for your payees and a secret code. To pay your bills, you call the bill-payer phone number, dial the account number and secret code, and enter each payee code and payment amount.

These services operate 24 hours a day and some even have toll-free 800 telephone numbers so you can make payments while out of town. There is a monthly fee for this service.

W.C. FIELDS

W.C. Fields, whom many regard as the greatest comic of all time, was born William Claude Dukinfield in 1879 in Philadelphia. He was the son of a London cockney who migrated to Philadelphia in the late 1870s. When Fields was eleven, he ran away from home and became a pilferer, juggler, vaudeville comic, and eventually a famous movie star. He had many unusual characteristics: he often drank two martinis before breakfast, he wrote two screenplays, *The Bank Dick* and *My Little Chickadee*, on the back of envelopes, and he yelled at his plants if they didn't bloom fast enough. He also had a fondness for made-up names: his last motion picture, *Never Give a Sucker an Even Break*, was written under the pen name Otis Criblecoblis. Two other pen names he liked were Mahatma Kane Jeeves and Charles Bogle.

W.C. Fields had more bank accounts than pen names—hundreds of bank accounts. It all began in Columbus, Ohio, when he was nineteen and earning $125 a week in vaudeville. It was a huge sum of money for a kid in those days. He had one bank account at the time but it was in California, too far to travel to make a deposit. So he devised a scheme to open a bank account everywhere he went. He began with large cities, depositing twenty dollars in one bank, ten in another, working his way down eventually to tiny banks

that were just a corner in a local feed store. He also loved jumping off trains and opening an account while the engineer took on more water. Fields tossed all his bankbooks in his wardrobe trunk and seemingly forgot about them, although Robert Lewis Taylor, who wrote a biography of the great comedian, said that several times Fields reviewed his books and cleaned out some of the accounts.

At one point, Fields told a friend he had 700 accounts in banks all over the world. When he died, his executors found thirty of them. Although many of Fields's accounts were in his own name, he also used madeup names such as Figley E. Whitesides, Sneed Hearn, Dr. Otis Guelpe, and Professor Curtis T. Bascom. Some think Fields's money may still be lying in accounts under phony names.

Fields established this unique savings system to discourage thievery and to be prepared in the event he was ever stranded somewhere without money. He constantly worried about being poor, perhaps because as a child he had so very little money. He once said that he often dreamed of being penniless and starving to death. The bank accounts helped dilute this fear.

Fields, who died on Christmas Day, 1946, left his money to establish an orphanage "Where no religion of any sort is to be preached."

W.C. Fields

Bank vaults keep money safely locked away.

HOW SAFE IS YOUR MONEY?

s unbelievable as it may seem, banks sometimes fail. Although we no longer have the huge panics that we did in the early part of this century, banks still have to close their doors from time to time. During the 1980s, a number of savings and loan institutions ran into financial difficulty and were merged or liquidated. It could happen again. So protect your money by using a bank that carries **insurance** and understanding precisely what that insurance covers.

Insurance: Protection against loss. A bank depositor's money is protected by the FDIC.

Insurance on Deposits

Most of our commercial banks are insured by the Federal Deposit Insurance Corporation (FDIC). You may have seen these initials on the window or front door of a bank. The FDIC is an independent government agency. In order to be a member of the

FDIC, a bank must meet certain standards and be examined periodically by federal and state agencies. Member banks pay insurance fees to the FDIC. The FDIC invests these fees in safe government securities. This money makes up the insurance funds that are used to cover depositor's accounts. In an emergency, the FDIC can add to these funds by borrowing from the U.S. Treasury.

Savings and loan: A financial institution that traditionally was limited to accepting savings deposits and making home mortgage loans. In recent years, S&Ls, also called "thrifts," have expanded their services.

Most **savings and loans**, sometimes called "thrifts," up until August 1989, were insured by the Federal Savings and Loan Insurance Corporation (FSLIC). That corporation ran into serious trouble and was declared insolvent—it didn't have enough money to do business. Now these institutions are insured by the Savings Association Insurance Fund (SAIF). SAIF is administered by FSLIC. The few S&Ls that are insured either by state insurance or private insurance do not have the backing of the government. Nor do the handful of savings banks that carry absolutely no insurance.

Protect your bank account by:

• Banking only at a federally insured institution. Look for the FDIC or SAIF sign at the bank.

• Keeping track of how much money is in your account. Individuals, not accounts, are insured up to $100,000, including interest and principal. That means if you have three accounts at the same bank in the same name, each with $100,000, you are insured only for a total of $100,000, not $300,000.

• If you ever have more than $100,000 you can extend the $100,000 cap by opening accounts in joint ownership with each of your parents.

• Moving your money. When the day comes that you have close to $100,000 in a bank account, move some of it to another bank to keep it fully insured. And remember, the interest the account earns will eventually take it over the $100,000 insurance cap.

To learn more about bank account insurance, contact the appropriate agency, listed in the Appendix.

Checking Up on Your Bank's Financial Health

In the future, you may have sizeable personal and business deposits with one or several banks. When that is the case, it will be worth your while to investigate the financial condition of the banks involved. There are several sources that will help you do this.

1) The bank itself. Get a copy of the bank's annual report and review it with an accountant. Among the points to look for are how high its **loan portfolio** is, how rapidly it is expanding, and its sources of income.

Loan portfolio: The collection of loans a bank has made to others.

2) Veribanc, Inc.
   P.O. Box 2963
   Woburn, MA 01888
   617-245-8370

This company will evaluate any bank for a modest fee.

3) FDIC
   C.S.B. Disclosure Group
   Room F-518
   550 17th Street, N.W.
   Washington, D.C. 20429
   202-393-8400

This group provides a paper entitled "Report of Condition" on banks (not individual branches), telling how much the bank is making, what its loan portfolio is made of, and what percentage of its loans are **nonperforming**. The cost of these reports is $2.40.

Nonperforming loan: A problem loan; one that is currently not paying interest.

Spotting Counterfeit Money

The various Federal Reserve Banks have high-speed equipment that electronically sorts and counts currency and in the process detects counterfeit money. The currency, in stacks up to 10,000 notes, is loaded onto a shelf on the side of a hugh machine. The notes are automatically fed into the sorter. As the currency moves through the machine, the de-

COUNTERFEITING THROUGH THE AGES

Counterfeiting is the illegal reproduction and distribution of a country's currency, coins, postage stamps, or bonds. In the United States, somewhere between $7 million and $11 million worth of counterfeit bills are made in a year. Much of this counterfeit is seized by government officials before it makes its way into circulation.

The great advances in offset printing and photographic processes make it much easier to make a close copy of money today than in the past. The typical counterfeiter runs off the bills at night or on weekends, sells them at a discount, say for twenty to twenty-five cents on the dollar, to criminal wholesalers who in turn sell the bills for thirty to forty cents to "passers." Individual counterfeiters are usually more successful than group operators because they work alone and are less likely to be caught. One of the most successful solo operators was Samuel Ninger, a sign painter. He made and distributed over $40,000 worth of hand-drawn bills between 1882 and 1896.

Counterfeiting is nothing new. When paper money was introduced in the colonies, counterfeiters quickly appeared on the scene. The first one we have a record of was Thomas Odell of Boston. In 1705 he counterfeited Massachusetts notes and then tried to pass them in Pennsylvania. He was sentenced to a year in prison and fined 300 pounds. Another early counterfeiter was James Mar, a skillful New York engraver. He was sentenced to be hanged, but the governor granted him clemency. A husband and wife team, Edward and Martha Hunt of Philadelphia, were caught counterfeiting in 1720. Edward was sentenced to death but his wife received a less harsh punishment—life imprisonment.

At various times throughout history, governments have actually allowed counterfeiting, especially during wartime. During the American Revolution, for example, the British counterfeited Continental currency, helping it become practically worthless. The largest wartime counterfeiting on record, "Operation Bernhard," was done by Nazi Germany during World War II. Some

nomination of each note is confirmed and counted and the quality is checked. A light reflector is used. The dirtier the money, the less light is reflected. Notes that are considered possible counterfeits are then redirected and examined by hand. About 35 counterfeit notes are found each day by the New York Federal Reserve Bank.

$630 million worth of bogus British pound notes were made in an effort to collapse the British economy and force them to give up without a fight. After 1942, some of it was used to pay off spies. During World War II, the U.S. Office of Stategic Services counterfeited Japanese yen notes.

At the time of the Civil War, as much as one-third of all paper money in circulation was believed to be counterfeit. This led to the establishment of the U.S. Secret Service to combat the crime.

In 1967, the Secret Service caught a fourteen-year-old boy who had been making $1 bills by photocopying them and pasting the two sides together. He used the

Secret Service agent displays counterfeit money.

bogus bills to get coins from a money changing machine at an automatic laundry. The manufacturers of these machines altered them so this can no longer be done.

The most recent trend is called desktop counterfeiting. It can be done with a personal computer and the proper software. Counterfeiters use an optical scanner to turn a legal document into a digital image, which is stored in the computer. Then, using a paint program, the counterfeiter changes the image—perhaps making the amount on a check larger or changing the name. The document is then printed out on a laser printer or on a typesetting machine.

Credit cards allow you the convenience of delaying payment.

CREDIT CARDS

credit, paying for things after you have them, is a major part of our daily lives. You see the use of credit all around you. When your dentist cleans your teeth, he or she may send your parents a bill for this work, giving them 30 days in which to pay. This is called extending credit. If, when you go to college, you take out a loan to help pay the tuition, this too is credit. So is the **mortgage** your parents may have on your house. They borrowed a large sum of money from the bank to purchase the house and each month they pay part of that loan, known as the mortgage, back to the bank.

Mortgage: A loan made by an institution to a homeowner; the homeowner pledges his or her home as collateral against the loan. The lender, usually a bank, may take possession of the home if the borrower does not pay back the loan as agreed.

Types of Credit Cards

The most common type of credit is a credit card, sometimes called "plastic." Maybe you've seen your parents use an American Express, Diners Club,

Visa or MasterCard. With these little plastic cards you can buy meals at fancy restaurants, clothes at the Gap, or tapes and CDs at Record World. Credit cards can even be used to buy tickets to concerts, the World Series, and the Super Bowl. Some credit cards are free; others have an annual fee. Credit cards are not issued to kids except with parental permission and then usually only as part of the parents' account. But, you should know all about them for the day when you have your own or when you use your parents'.

• ***Retail credit cards.*** Local department stores and oil companies, which issue credit cards for use in their own stores or stations, do not have annual fees. In fact, these cards cost nothing to use, as long as you pay your bill promptly. If you pay only part of the bill when it is due, then you face a finance charge, which is a certain interest rate on the unpaid amount. This rate is often extremely high—and has reached 18 percent and 20 percent recently.

• ***Bank credit cards.*** Bank cards, such as Visa and MasterCard, are issued by individual banks. Visa and MasterCard provide advertising, credit authorization, and record keeping for the banks. Most bank cards charge an annual fee. These cards can be used in a wide range of places—hotels, airlines, stores, restaurants, etc. You have a choice of paying your entire bill within the due period (usually a month), in which case there is no interest charge, or you can pay your bill over time, in

Installments: Payments for an item which are made over a designated time period rather than all at once.

installments, in which case a sizeable interest charge is added to the balance due. Banks can, within broad terms, charge whatever interest they like and set whatever payment terms they like. It's important to understand that fact because it means all credit cards are definitely not alike.

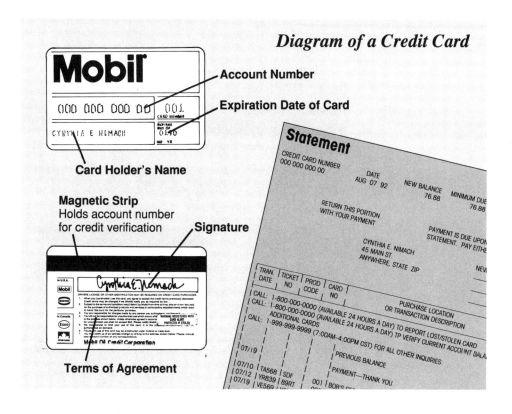

Diagram of a Credit Card

The monthly statement or bill indicates the full amount you have charged during the billing period, where you made each purchase, and the date each item was purchased. As you can see in the example above, the statement also gives the interest rate and the minimum amount due. If you decide to pay for your purchases in installments rather than all at once, you must at least pay this minimum amount every month. If the annual percentage rate is 10 percent, then you are paying $10 on every $100 borrowed. If it's 18.5 percent, then it costs $18.50 to borrow $100. Credit card issuers must tell borrowers what this rate is.

Bank credit cards such as Visa and MasterCard make money by charging credit card holders an annual fee, charging interest on unpaid balances, and charging retailers a commission for converting charges into cash.

Bank cards are issued with a preset spending limit. That is the maximum dollar amount you can charge. This figure, determined by the bank that issues the card, is sometimes called a line of credit. It is based on how much income you have and your credit history—whether you pay your bills on time or not. The line of credit could be $500 or $5,000, or some other amount.

Once you have spent up to this limit, sometimes called a cap, you cannot charge any additional items. Of course, you should never allow yourself to reach this limit. But if you do, your card will be rejected by retailers.

• ***Travel and entertainment cards.*** Diners Club, American Express, and Carte Blanche cards, known as T&Es, require full payment at the end of the billing period.

• ***Premium cards.*** These special so-called status cards have higher annual fees in return for slightly lower interest rates, higher credit lines, and occasional special offerings. American Express has a gold and a platinum premium card. Visa and MasterCard also have premium cards.

• ***Debit cards.*** This card is neither a credit nor a T&E card, yet it has some similarities. A debit card does not offer credit at all. Instead, when you make a purchase, the cost of that purchase is instantly deducted from your checking account balance. The advantage is that you do not have to write checks for these charges. The disadvantage is that if your checking account earns interest, you lose interest for the two or three days that it takes for a personal check to clear.

Using Your Parents' Credit Card

When you're old enough to do your own shopping, your parents may feel comfortable letting you use a credit card to pay for your purchases. If so, they are saying, "we trust you to be reasonable with money." When you go off to college or move away from home, they may want you to have a credit card for emergencies. But don't expect unlimited use of a credit card. And even if it's offered, don't abuse the privilege.

Playing Your Cards Right

Before you use a credit card, you and your parents should draw up reasonable guidelines for its use:

1) Determine if the card is to pay for a specific purchase, such as a pair of boots. If it is, establish the price range. Is it $25 to $35 or $25 to $75? Without a predetermined price range, you may buy an expensive pair of Italian leather boots when your parents had galoshes in mind. Setting price ranges eliminates potential confusion and arguments.

2) Make a list of the types of items or situations in which the credit card can be used. Even if you don't have a credit card now, you probably will in the future and then, too, you should restrict its use. Among the items students often use credit cards for: gasoline, car repairs, clothing, sports equipment, special meals out, and airline tickets.

3) Decide who will pay for what charges. Will all items charged on the card be paid for by your parents? By you? Or, will you share paying? If you share, what items are your responsibility?

4) Decide if use of the card is permanent or limited. Do you have permission to carry it all the time in your wallet or purse, or do you ask for it when you need it?

He who is without cash in pocket might as well be buried in a ricetub with his mouth sewed up.

—Chinese proverb

Protecting Your Card

• Write the credit card number and the issuer (American Express, local department store) on an index card or in your budget notebook. See page 108 for how to set up this notebook. If you lose your credit card or it is stolen, call the issuer immediately. The issuer's telephone number, often a toll-free one, is usually listed on the monthly statement. If you do not have a statement, call the 800 information operator or the bank that issued the card if it is a bank card.

• When you receive a new card, either because the old one expired or you requested a replacement, cut the old one in several sections with a pair of scissors and sign the new one immediately.

• Never sign a blank charge slip.

• Tear up all carbons and incorrect charge slips. These can be used by thieves to obtain your name and account number.

• Do not give your account number over the phone unless you have called to make a purchase.

• Save your charge slips and compare them with your monthly statement; report unauthorized charges at once.

• Never lend your card to anyone, not even your best friend.

Advantages of Credit Cards

Although much emphasis must be placed on not abusing credit and credit cards, perhaps because so many people have trouble and go on spending binges with plastic, these cards, when used wisely, have many advantages.

• You don't have to carry large amounts of cash.

• You can take advantage of sale items.

• You get detailed, monthly reports on what you purchase.

• You receive one bill for a number of items.

• You can easily purchase items by mail order.

- Many merchants prefer credit cards to personal checks.
- They serve as proof of your identity.
- They enable you to make and guarantee hotel reservations by phone or fax.
- You can obtain cash advances, especially useful when in a foreign country.
- Credit cards are almost universally required for renting a car or van.
- You build up a good credit history, which will help you obtain bank loans in the future.

Big Brother: Your Credit File and What's in It

How do Visa, American Express, and your local department store know whether or not to give you a credit card? They check your credit reputation with a **credit bureau**. Credit bureaus, which are independent businesses, maintain credit histories on thousands of people. They gather, store, and sell information to credit grantors (banks, American Express, etc.) and other paying subscribers. There are about 2,000 such bureaus across the country keeping track of the financial habits of millions of Americans.

Credit bureau: A business that solicits, files, and dispenses information on people's financial habits, especially how they pay their bills and loans.

In urban areas, files are maintained by one of the five big bureaus: Trans Union, Chilton, CBI, Associated Credit Services, and TRW. In smaller cities and towns, local bureaus are used. (See Appendix for telephone numbers.)

Credit bureaus do not decide who should get credit and who should not. They are merely depositories for information, although credit decisions are often made based on what is in someone's file.

These files contain data on whether people pay their bills on time; if they are late and if so, how late; if they have declared bankruptcy; if they are behind in their tax payments; and if they have been denied credit by another credit card issuer or a bank. Criminal convictions and civil law suits are also included. They keep a scorecard of where a person has obtained credit, how that person pays his or her bills, and how much he or she now owes. There is nothing about your life style, political inclinations, or religion.

This information comes from creditors who subscribe to the credit bureau and send in reports on their clients, other creditors who supply information at your request, and publicly recorded court documents, such as tax liens or bankruptcy records.

You have a right to know what's in your file as well as who else has seen it for credit reasons in the last six months. If you request your file within 30 days after you have been denied credit, you cannot be charged a fee. For all other requests, the credit bureau may charge you a fee of $3 to $30.

• *Who can see your file?* Not just anyone can peek into your file. The federal Fair Credit Reporting Act protects your privacy. It states that your file can be given *only* to a person the bureau believes will use the information in connection with a credit transaction.

• *Tracking down your report.* Once you begin to build up a credit history, you should check your file once a year and report any errors to the appropriate bureau. If any information is missing, you can ask that it be added. To find the bureau that has your report, check in the Yellow Pages under "Credit Reporting Agencies." If that doesn't work, call your bank or a department store where you have a charge account and ask for the name of the bureau it uses. Or call the five large bureaus mentioned in this chapter. When you phone the bureau, have a pencil and paper handy. Many use taped

THE LARGEST CREDIT CARD COLLECTION

The largest number of valid credit cards is owned by Walter Cavanagh of Santa Clara, CA.   Known as "Mr. Plastic Fantastic," he has 1,208 different cards. | He keeps them in the world's longest wallet, which measures 250 feet long and weighs 35 pounds.—(1990 Guinness Book of World Records)

messages explaining how to get a copy of your report. You will probably be asked to send a letter stating your name, address, telephone number, Social Security number, and the names of your credit cards. Some credit bureaus send a form for you to fill out instead.

Your First Credit Card

Although you may not be old enough to apply for your own credit card, you will be within several years. Sometimes students and those just out of school encounter difficulty in getting their first credit card because they lack a work history and/or substantial income. Here are five tips to help you to get your first card.

1) Banks and other credit card issuers frequently send solicitation letters to college students, especially those with jobs or those about to graduate. If your application is approved, it's an easy way to get your first card. However, more favorable rates are probably available elsewhere. After you are established in a full-time job with regular income, you can switch to a card with a lower annual fee and/or lower interest rates.

2) If you cannot get a major credit card, start small. Open a charge account at your local drugstore or hardware store. Charge items and pay for them within 30 days. This establishes you as a good credit risk.

HOW TO FIND THE BEST CREDIT CARD

Bankcard Holders of America, a nonprofit consumer organization, continually surveys credit card issuers and makes their results available to the public.

• For a list of credit cards with low interest, request "Low Interest Credit Card List," and send $1.50.

• For a list of credit cards with no annual fees, request "No Annual Fee Credit Card List," and send $1.50.

• For a copy of "How to Choose a Credit Card," send $1.00 to
Bankcard Holders of America
Herndon Parkway
Suite 120
Herndon, VA 22070

3) Contact a bank offering a secured credit card. Under this plan, you deposit money, say $1,000, in a savings account and use it as collateral for paying your monthly bills on a credit card that the bank issues. Your deposit earns interest but usually you cannot withdraw this money without giving up your credit card.

4) Take out a personal loan at your bank, even if it's only several hundred dollars, and pay it back on time. This establishes you as a good credit risk.

5) Answer all the questions on the application. If a question does not apply to your situation, write in "not applicable." Unanswered questions are considered negative by loan officers.

Picking the Best Card

When you do shop for a credit card, do just that—shop. There are many differences between cards. Here are the three factors you should weigh.

1) *Interest rate.* To find the best rate, call several issuers and watch for news about them in the financial magazines and the newspaper. This rate is especially crucial if you do not pay your bill within the 30-day time period.

2) *Annual fee.* Not all cards have annual fees. If you pay your bill in full within the stated time period, then the interest rate is not important, but the annual fee is. You should select a low or no fee card.

3) *Grace periods.* Cards with no grace period begin calculating interest on all purchases as soon as they appear on the statement. Other card issuers give 30 days after purchase before interest charges are applied.

If You Slide into Deep Debt

It's unlikely that as a student you will find yourself in serious debt. However, after you finish school and are holding down a job, it's possible. Thousands of Americans at some time in their lives find themselves faced with mounting bills. A sudden

---

THE LEADING CREDIT BUREAUS

Trans Union Credit Information Co.
444 North Michigan
Chicago, IL 60611

CSC Credit Services, Inc.
652 North Belt East
Houston, TX 77060

Chilton Corp.
12606 Greenville Avenue
Dallas, TX 75243

Equifax, Inc.
The Credit Bureau, Inc.
P.O. Box 4091
Atlanta, GA 30302

TRW Information Services
505 City Parkway West
P.O. Box 5450
Orange, CA 92667

illness, being fired, having to help out someone else—many things make it difficult for people to pay their bills on time. Should this ever happen to you, don't hide the fact. Seek help. Follow the advice of the **Federal Trade Commission**.

Federal Trade Commission (FTC): A federal agency established in 1914 that fosters free and fair business competition and at the same time protects consumers.

Although the Commission does not solve individual problems, it suggests that people who need help in dealing with debt contact a Consumer Credit Counseling Service. This nonprofit organization has offices throughout the country. CCCS counselors try to arrange a repayment plan that is acceptable to you and your creditors. These services are offered at little or no charge.

To find the nearest CCCS office, contact:

National Foundation for Consumer Credit, Inc.
Suite 601
8701 Georgia Avenue
Silver Spring, MD 20910
301-589-5600

The Federal Trade Commission enforces a number of laws involving consumer credit and has free fact sheets explaining these laws. Useful publications include "Fair Credit Reporting Act," "Fair Credit Billing Act," "Women and Credit Histories," and "Solving Credit Problems."

To order these publications, contact:

Public Reference
Federal Trade Commission
6th and Pennsylvania Avenue, NW
Washington, D.C. 20580
202-523-3598

DINERS CLUB: THE FIRST TRAVEL & ENTERTAINMENT CARD

Dustin Hoffman, who plays a college graduate in the movie *The Graduate*, is told by the father of one of his friends that he should consider a career in "plastics." The well-meaning father may not have been referring to plastic charge cards, but perhaps he should have. Credit cards have been one of the country's fastest growing businesses because, at one time or another, most Americans own a credit card.

It all began in 1950, when an American businessman and his guests went to a popular New York restaurant for dinner. They had a wonderful time and an excellent meal. When the check came, the host reached for his wallet. He had no cash. The man was Frank McNamara.

Mr. McNamara discussed the situation with the restaurant. They agreed to let him pay later, and he resolved never to let this embarassment happen again. His resolution brought about an innovation that affected the economic behavior of millions of people.

Soon after that evening out, McNamara and an attorney conceived the idea of a charge card and on February 28, 1950, the first multi-use charge card was issued. Called a Diners Club Card, it was accepted in just twenty-seven dining establishments. During that first year, only 200 people, mostly Mr. McNamara's friends, carried the card. The annual fee was just $5. By early 1951, the number of card members had grown to over 42,000 and over $1 million had been charged through 330 restaurants, hotels, nightclubs, and a handful of retailers.

In 1952, Alfred Bloomingdale, the department store heir, was so impressed that he invested $25,000 in the growing business. Diners Club was first accepted by a car rental agency in 1952 and by 1959, Hertz, Avis, and National joined in. Soon gasoline stations accepted the card, along with thousands of motels.

Only three years after its introduction, Diners Club became the first international travel and entertainment card—used in the United Kingdom, Canada, Cuba, and Mexico. By 1960, the card was honored in over fifty countries. Western Airlines was the first airline to accept a charge card, and it was a Diners Club Card. In 1980, it became the first travel and entertainment card honored in the People's Republic of China. Diners Club also introduced the first travel insurance available through a charge card. Today, through its Club Assistance Emergency Service, emergency medical, legal, and travel help is available twenty-four hours a day, seven days a week, anywhere in the world for cardholders. Many other credit and travel and entertainment cards have followed the example set by Frank McNamara.

The first Diners' Club Card.

INVESTMENT SAVINGS ACCOUNTS

	CURRENT RATE		ANNUAL YIELD*	
1 YEAR TAX FREE 'ALL SAVERS' CD $500 MINIMUM DEPOSIT	**9.523**	%	**9.990**	%
30 MONTH CD $500 MINIMUM DEPOSIT	**14.00**	%	**15.248**	%
3½ YEAR FIXED RATE CD $500 MINIMUM DEPOSIT	**13.900**	%	**14.820**	%

DRY DOCK SAVINGS BANK

Banks are very competitive and often promote their special services.

INVESTMENT OPPORTUNITIES AT YOUR BANK

Your bank does more than just offer savings and checking accounts. It has several investment-type accounts in which you can earn a higher rate of interest than is paid on a savings account. The only hitch is that most require a minimum of $500 to $1,000 or more. The one exception is savings bonds, which are sold for as little as $25. Technically these are not a bank account; they are bonds sold by the Bureau of Public Debt through banks.

When you have accumulated a substantial amount in your savings account, you're ready to make the switch from saver to investor. In this chapter we will look at the three key investments offered at most banks: savings bonds, money market deposit accounts, and certificates of deposits (CDs). Then we will talk briefly about using your bank to buy stocks, bonds, and mutual funds.

Savings Bonds

These bonds, officially called EE Savings Bonds, are one of the safest and least expensive investments you can buy. They are backed by our government and they start at just $25. Savings bonds are sold at a 50 percent discount from face value, so a $50 bond actually costs only $25; a $100, only $50. Bonds are sold in denominations ranging from $50 to $10,000.

Unlike a savings account in which you receive interest on a regular basis, you do not receive interest on these bonds until you turn them in (called redeeming). That's because the difference between the discount price and the face value constitutes the interest. The government guarantees that the rate on bonds held five years or longer won't fall below 6 percent. The longer a bond is held, the more interest it earns. The interest rate on the bonds changes every six months: May 1 and November 1. To get the current rate call 800-US-BONDS. When you buy savings bonds at your bank there is no fee or transaction cost.

In addition to being tops in safety, these bonds have certain tax advantages. You (or your parents) will not have to pay state and local taxes on the interest earned, and if your parents purchased bonds after January 1, 1989 and use them to pay for your college tuition, they may not have to pay federal taxes. (See Chapter 11 for more details.)

Money Market Deposit Accounts

These accounts, which go by diferent names at different banks (Money Management Account, Market Plus, etc.), offer liquidity, fairly high interest rates, and safety. Although interest rates and minimum dollar requirements vary from bank to bank, in general, money market accounts earn 5.25

percent up to a certain balance. Above that level, the interest rate rises to what is called the market interest rate. The market interst rate fluctuates (daily or weekly, depending upon the bank) but it is higher than the rates paid on savings and NOW accounts. Because there's no legal requirement or restriction on what rate banks can pay on these accounts, you should shop around for the best rates.

You can write three checks per month on this type of acount; if you write more you will be penalized, generally $5 to $10 per check. However, you can take your money out—some or all of it—at any time.

A money market account, then, is a cross between a savings and checking account. Like a savings account, your money earns interest, but the interest rate changes whereas in a savings account it remains the same. As with a checking account, you can write checks, but only three per month without a penalty.

Certificates of Deposit

A certificate of deposit (CD) is a promissory note that you receive from a bank in return for loaning the bank money. When you purchase a CD, the bank promises to pay you a fixed rate of interest, (a few CDs have fluctuating rates) for a set time period. At the end of that time period, you will get back the full amount of your loan (called the principal) plus interest.

The interest rates on CDs vary widely from bank to bank. For convenience you may want to use your own bank. But if you'd like to be more adventuresome, check the list of the nation's highest yielding CDs that appears every Friday in *The Wall Street Journal*. If rates are significantly higher, you may want to buy an out-of-town CD. But before

Maturity: Date on which the principal amount of a bond (the amount the bondholder loaned the issuer) becomes due and must be paid back to the bondholder.

Stock: Ownership in a corporation that is represented by a stock certificate.

Bond: An IOU issued by a corporation, a municipality, or the U.S. government. The issuer promises to pay the bondholder, who has made the loan, a specified rate of interest for a certain period of time. When that time period is up, the bond matures and the bondholder receives the full face value back, i.e., the amount loaned.

Mutual fund: An investment company in which thousands of dollars from individual shareholders are pooled together to purchase stocks, bonds, and other investments. This money is managed by a professional portfolio manager.

you do, call the bank and ask if it is federally insured by FDIC or SAIF.

If you cash in your CD before it matures, there is an interest rate penalty, ranging form one month's to six month's interest or more. Therefore, don't invest in a CD if you think you might need the money before it **matures**. Use a money market deposit account instead, where you can take your money out at any time without a penalty. CDs have a variety of maturity lengths: the most common maturities are three months, six months, one year, three years, and five years. You can select the maturity that best suits your needs.

CDs also come in various dollar or principal amounts. The most popular are $500, $1,000, $2,500, and $5,000, although each bank can offer any amount it wishes.

Once you have enough money in your savings, consider purchasing a CD if the rates are higher than those on a money market deposit account and if you can tie up your money for the necessary time period.

Stocks, Bonds, and Mutual Funds

Many larger banks now have brokerage firm subsidiaries. A brokerage firm is a business that is authorized to sell **stocks**, **bonds**, and **mutual funds** to the public. Ask if your bank sells these securities and, if so, ask the bank for literature describing their service. You can learn all about these investments by reading other books in this series.

SAVINGS BONDS AND THE WAR EFFORT

The U.S. government sold War bonds to help pay for World War II. A great many groups worked hard to boost sales.

The first big War Bond drive took place in September 1942. Three hundred thirty-seven actors and actresses participated, often working eighteen hours a day. They visited 300 cities and towns as well as army camps all over the world, including those on the front lines.

One of the most famous participants was Dorothy Lamour, who, dressed in a sarong, sold $350,000,000 in bonds. Another actress, the beautiful Hedy Lamarr, kissed anyone who bought $25,000 worth of bonds. One man, so excited at the prospect, fainted before Hedy could actually kiss him. He took a raincheck.

It wasn't all fun: Greer Garson collapsed from exhaustion; Bette Davis had to rest up when it was over; and Rita Hayworth quit in the middle, also from exhaustion. And there was one great tragedy: Carole Lombard was killed in a plane crash.

The 1942 drive sold $838,540,000 worth of bonds, representing one-sixth of the total number of bonds sold.

In 1943, Secretary of the Treasury Henry Morgenthau launched a nationwide advertising campaign to sell War Bonds. Radio shows, milk bottle tops, and even matchbook covers contained such slogans as "Back the Attack" and "Buy E Bonds, the Little Man's Bond."

Baseball also contributed to the war effort and at some games, admission was a War Bond. The most famous of these was a three-way game held in New York between the Giants, Yankees, and Dodgers. Each team went to bat six times in the same nine-inning game against a rotating lineup. The final score was Dodgers 5, Yankees 1, and Giants 0.

Baseball also helped the war effort by donating money from the annual All-Star Game to purchase sports equipment for men in the service. And the fan's right to keep a ball hit by a player into the stands was suspended during the war. The fan was supposed to throw the ball back so it could be used by the soldiers. Anyone who didn't, or who dared hesitate, was booed by the fans, who chanted: "Throw it back, throw it back."

Actresses helping to sell war bonds.

Safe deposit boxes are for safe storage of valuables and important documents.

9

OTHER BANK SERVICES

D uring the last decade banks have expanded their operations beyond the traditional savings and checking accounts. You have already encountered some of those services in Chapters 6 and 8. Here are four other areas in which banks can be useful. Although you may not need these services while you are in school, you should be aware of them for the future.

Safe Deposit Boxes
These metal boxes, located in the bank's vault, are used to store valuables. They come in various sizes and can be rented for an annual fee. Only the person who has signed the appropriate signature card with the bank *and* has the key to the box may open the box. It takes two keys to open a box—the renter has one and the bank the other. Neither key will work alone.

Among the items kept in safe deposit boxes:
- valuable jewelry
- stock and bond certificates
- birth certificates
- marriage certificates
- deed to house or property
- copies of wills
- proof of valuables, such as pictures of heirlooms and art

Do not keep items that might be needed should the person who rents the box dies, such as his or her will, life insurance policies, cemetery deed or burial instructions. The box may be sealed shut upon the death of the owner and it may take a court order to remove these documents. State rules vary, so check first before putting in vital documents and before renting a box jointly with someone else.

Special Checks

- *Traveler's checks.* As a convenience to customers, most banks sell traveler's checks, usually for a nominal fee. Use these instead of cash when traveling. If traveler's checks are lost or stolen, you will get your money back.

- *Certified checks.* A certified check is a personal check that has been stamped "certified" by the bank after funds have been set aside from your account to cover the full amount of this check. You almost always need a certified check when buying a house or other property.

- *Cashier's checks.* If you don't have a checking account but need a guarantee of payment, you can give the bank money and it will make out a check to the person you designate.

- *Money orders.* Money orders are a simple way to transfer small amounts of money without using a check or cash. The money order is similar in appearance to a check: it has the name of the purchaser, the name of the person who is to get the money, and the amount to be paid. To get a money

A bank is a place that will lend you money if you can prove you don't need it.

—Bob Hope, 1967

order you give the bank cash for the amount plus a small fee. (Money orders are also available at post offices.)

Help for Wealthy Clients

Most major banks and some smaller ones operate private banking divisions and trust departments. Private banking divisions attend to the needs of those handling large sums of money. A bank officer is often assigned to take care of that person's needs.

Trust departments, often headed by an attorney, administer trusts and investments. They carry out all the provisions of a **trust**, administer wills, and sell **estates** if necessary. They also invest money or advise individuals about investing. Charges for these services are high.

Loans

Certain items in life cost more than most of us can save for at one time—houses, condominiums, cars, boats, and college education, just to name a few. When the day comes that you want to purchase something you cannot afford, you have the option of borrowing money to pay for it. However, such a decision should not be made without serious thought. Thousands of Americans have borrowed to finance a major purchase only to discover they were unable to make the loan payments on time. They then are said to be "drowning in debt." However, going into debt, prudently and carefully, can help achieve financial and personal goals that are otherwise almost impossible.

When you need a loan, review your income and other obligations with your banker. Make a thoughtful decision, not an emotional one. You will have several basic types of loans to consider:

Trust: A legal relationship in which a person, called the trustee, holds property, investments or money for someone else, called the beneficiary.

Estate: All the things one owns at the time of death. An estate can consist of real estate, stocks, bonds, money, a business or part of a business, furniture, jewelry, paintings, cars, and so forth. One's estate is distributed to heirs and others according to directions left in a will or, if there is no will, by court ruling.

MAJOR TYPES OF LOANS

Automobile loan: A loan available from banks, auto manufacturers, and auto dealers for the purpose of buying a car, truck, or van. The car serves as collateral.

Credit card loan: An advance against your credit card; also called a line of credit. It is often open-ended, that is, as long as you make regular payments, additional loan money is available.

Home equity loan: A revolving line of credit, offered by banks allowing homeowners to borrow at will on the built-up equity (ownership) in their home. The house serves as collateral and can be sold by the bank if the borrower fails to pay off the loan.

Mortgage: A loan obtained by pledging property such as a house or apartment as collateral or security for the loan. The bank can sell the property if the borrower does not pay back the mortgage. Mortgage payments are usually made monthly until the loan is paid in full. Mortgages can run as long as 30 years.

Personal loan: Loan obtained from a bank, family, or friends. It is often unsecured, which means no collateral is pledged. Some banks offer secured personal loans in which the borrower's savings account, CD, stocks, or bonds are pledged as collateral.

Note: Interest on loans is either fixed—in which case it is the same for a certain period, often the entire length of the loan, or it is variable—in which case it increases or decreases depending upon overall interest rates.

mortgages, automobile loans, personal loans, secured savings loans, home equity loans, and credit cards. While we cannot discuss each of these in depth in this book, these are the key guidelines to keep in mind when shopping for a loan:

1) What is the interest rate? Will that rate remain in effect for the entire loan period? Or will it fluctuate? If it fluctuates, how high can it go? And how often can it be changed?

2) What are the monthly payments? What happens if I cannot make a monthly payment?

3) After making the monthly payment, how much money will I have left over from my paycheck?

4) What will happen to my loan if I should become ill or die?

5) What will be the total cost of this loan (interest and principal) by the time it is paid off?

6) How many years do I have to pay off this loan?

7) Can I pay it off early?

8) Is any of the interest tax deductible?

9) What fees are involved in taking out this loan?

A VERY RICH CHILD

When Christina Onassis, the daughter of the famous Greek shipping magnate, Aristotle Onassis, died near Buenos Aires, Argentina in November, 1988, she left her daughter, Athina, a fortune estimated at over a billion dollars. This has made Athina one of the world's richest people. Among her many possessions are a private zoo at her villa near Geneva, fleets of ships, skyscrapers around the world, and the beautiful Ionian island of Skorpios in Greece. Four men associated with the Onassis Group, the parent company that oversees all the family's enterprises, and Athina's father will manage her fortune until she is an adult.

Athina Onassis

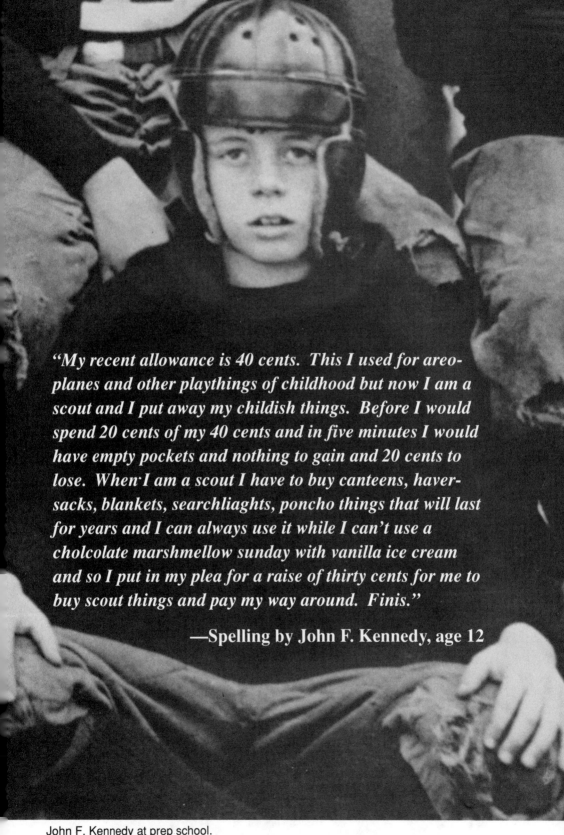

*"My recent allowance is 40 cents. This I used for areo-
planes and other playthings of childhood but now I am a
scout and I put away my childish things. Before I would
spend 20 cents of my 40 cents and in five minutes I would
have empty pockets and nothing to gain and 20 cents to
lose. When I am a scout I have to buy canteens, haver-
sacks, blankets, searchliaghts, poncho things that will last
for years and I can always use it while I can't use a
cholcolate marshmellow sunday with vanilla ice cream
and so I put in my plea for a raise of thirty cents for me to
buy scout things and pay my way around. Finis."*

—Spelling by John F. Kennedy, age 12

John F. Kennedy at prep school.

10

BUDGETING MADE FUN

Y our parents may give you a monthly or weekly allowance for you to spend as you like. Or they may request that you give some of it to your church, synagogue, or charitable organization. In some families, part of an allowance is for doing certain small jobs. Taking charge of your allowance and other money you receive from home is the best way to learn the techniques of money management. Here are some tips for getting the most out of this income.

1) *Think of your allowance as a paycheck.* Ask your parents to set a specific day when the allowance is distributed. Then you know each week you have the same amount of money coming in for the time period covered.

2) *Ask to receive it at the beginning or the middle of the week.* It's more tempting to spend

money on weekends. By getting your allowance at the early part of the week you'll learn to pace your spending. This will help prepare you for the day when you receive a paycheck on a monthly or bi-monthly basis, or if you work as a freelancer, on an intermittent basis.

3) *Discuss what your allowance is for with your parents.* Each family handles money in a different way. Know whether your allowance is just for fun things—movies, pizza, a trip to McDonald's—or if you are expected to use it for school lunches, bus fare, and clothes. Draw up a written agreement spelling out how this money is to be used.

4) *Don't ask for more if you've overspent.* If you race through your allowance on Saturday, don't expect your parents to bail you out on Sunday. Spending too much at one time was *your* decision. If, as a kid, you constantly turn to others to rescue you from poor money management, you may never learn to handle your paycheck as an adult.

5) *Prepare the facts when asking for a raise.* You may have legitimate needs for an increase in your allowance. Make a list and present it to your parents. For example, if you join the debate club or swim team, you may have to give up your after-school job, in which case you will need a little help from your parents. Or, if the cost of living has gone up and your allowance has not, you can have a reasonable case for an increase.

6) *Being paid for extra jobs.* Some parents pay kids for doing extra chores around the house—cleaning out the garage, washing the family car, mowing the lawn. If you would like to institute this practice in your family, explain that you want to earn money so you can be more independent financially. Draw up a list of jobs with an estimate of how much each job is worth. If your parents resist

the idea at first, don't push it. Bring it up later on; a new idea often takes time to implement. But your parents may simply not believe in paying you to do work for them. In that case, offer the same list of jobs to several of your neighbors. You may land yourself a weekend job. Whether or not you get paid for around-the-house tasks, don't expect to be paid for everything you do. Keeping your room clean and helping with the evening dishes are simply part of being a member of the family.

7) *Earning money outside your home.* If you have a part-time or summer job, set aside part of each paycheck for savings—even if it's just a few dollars. It's a good habit to learn and you'll be surprised at how easy it is once you've begun.

8) *Being paid for grades.* You should want to earn good grades for yourself. Don't expect to be paid for them.

Drawing Up a Mini-Budget

Never ask of money spent
Where the spender thinks it went.
Nobody was ever meant
To remember or invent
What he did with every cent.
—*Robert Frost*

The best way to get the most out of every cent is to keep a simple budget. You may want to write your budget in a special notebook designed for that purpose that is available at stationery stores. You also can use a spiral notebook. The following pages are examples of what might be useful to include in your notebook. You can also use it to keep track of interest rates, the numbers of your savings and checking accounts, and bank telephone numbers.

A budget helps you keep track of money as it comes in and as it goes out. It enables you to see

My Budget

Income

Allowance (weekly/monthly)	$_____
Odd jobs around the house	$_____
After-school job	$_____
Other	$_____
Total:	**$_____**

Fixed Expenses

School lunches	$_____
Bus fare	$_____
Church/synagogue contribution	$_____
Savings	$_____
Other	$_____
Total:	**$_____**

Flexible Expenses

Telephone calls	$_____
Snacks	$_____
Movies, concerts, events	$_____
Clothes	$_____
CDs, tapes	$_____
Presents/gifts	$_____
Other	$_____
Total:	**$_____**

where you spend your money and where you could spend less. Budgets can cover income and expenses for almost any time period. If you receive your allowance on a weekly basis, then draw up a weekly budget. Ideally, your income should cover your expenses, or at least the ones you are responsible for. When that is the case you are said to be in the "black." If your expenses are greater than your income, you're in the "red" and you need to cut back. Since fixed expenses are just that, fixed, cutting back has to take place among your flexible expenses.

The Savings Jar Trick

When you receive money from an allowance, a job, or as a gift, make it a hard and fast rule to always save some portion of it. Good savings habits should be in place by the time you are in junior high school. And don't wait for a parent or grandparent to talk you into it. Start now, on your own. After you move away from home, you and only you have the power to build up your savings. Like going on a diet or working out at the gym, no one else can do it for you, but the rewards at the end are great.

An easy way to begin is by taking three empty jars and labeling them: "Money for Fun," "Money for the Bank," and "Money for Things." Put one third of the money you get into each jar. When you have enough money in the Bank Jar, say $25 or $50, make a deposit in your bank account immediately so you can start earning interest. You may be tempted to raid the Bank Jar when you deplete the Fun Jar. *Don't!* The money that you save can be used later on for major things: college graduation, a car, a stereo or CD player. If you never fund your savings account, you'll always be stuck buying little things, often things that have limited use or pleasure, and never have enough for the big ones.

When you have a regular, full-time job, these same savings principles will still apply, only the labels will be different. Then you will be responsible for such items as rent or a mortgage on a house, clothing, food, telephone and electricity, college loans, and possibly a car. Many adults make the mistake of thinking that if they only earned more money they would be able to save. This simply isn't so. No matter how much or how little you earn, the concept of saving is the same, and that is: save something, 50 cents, $5, $500 or $5,000, on a regular basis.

Remember: Savings is spending deferred. It is only putting off satisfaction and pleasure, not denying it or throwing it away.

Easy Ways to Save

Benjamin Franklin reportedly said, "A penny saved is a penny earned." Today of course, a penny doesn't buy much; even penny candy and bubble gum costs more than a penny. But the concept is still as valid as when Franklin said it. Here are some simple savings techniques to adopt at various stages of your life. Some will work well now; others when you are in college or working steadily.

1) Put money aside before you spend it. Pretend that saving is just one of your monthly bills. Put cash in your savings jar or write out a check to deposit in your savings account before you allocate money for other things.

2) Begin by saving 1 percent of your income each month. That can be 1 percent of your allowance, 1 percent from an after school or summer job, or 1 percent of any other sources of income you may have. Then try to increase that amount by 1 percent a month. By the end of the year you'll be saving 12 percent per month!

3) Take advantage of automatic savings plans. You can't save money you never see. Have money automatically transferred into a savings account from your checking account, or, when you're working, from your paycheck.

4) Save your change at the end of the day. When you get home after school or work, put one type of coin into a container. When these small amounts add up to $10 or $20, take them to your bank.

5) Pay off credit cards. If you're using a credit card, pay your bill in full each month. Interest charges are very high and interest payments as of 1991 aren't tax deductible.

6) Keep making payments. If you ever take out a loan and then pay it off, continue to write the

Regarding inflation: A nickel goes a long way now. You can carry it around for days without finding a thing it will buy.

—American saying

same check (or at least half that amount) and stash it in your savings account. You became accustomed to living without this money, so now you can exchange debt for savings and head toward making the "Ten Richest" list.

Your Net Worth

You've probably heard people say, "Oh, he's worth millions," or "She's one of the richest women in the world." They are talking about a person's net worth. You, too, have a net worth, although as a student it probably won't get you on the country's "Ten Richest" list.

Figuring out your net worth every year helps you keep tabs on your savings, investing, and spending patterns. It enables you to see if it has gone up, which hopefully it has, or if you're losing ground, and it has declined. If that's the case, you need to reevaluate your budget. Perhaps you're not saving enough. Maybe you need to ask for a raise, or change jobs. Maybe you've spent too much on luxury items. Or maybe it's simply because you've gone back to school and are temporarily earning less. Tracking your net worth forces you to look at your financial profile.

Figure your net worth using the worksheet on the next page. Some of the categories will not be applicable until you are working, so just fill in the ones for which you have answers.

Keeping Financial Records

Add your net worth statement to your budget book. If you keep these records up to date until you graduate from high school, you will have a sound idea of how you're handling your money—maybe even a better one than the adults in your life. It's

WORKSHEET

Date_____

ASSETS

Cash on hand	$_____
(including allowance)	
Cash in checking accounts	$_____
Savings accounts	$_____
Money market accounts/	$_____
funds	
Life insurance, cash value	$_____
Annuities	$_____

Retirement funds
IRA or Keogh	$_____
Vested interest in pension or	$_____
profit-sharing plan	
U.S. savings bonds	$_____
Market value of stocks	$_____
Market value of bonds	$_____
Market value of mutual funds	$_____

Property (value if sold)
Automobile	$_____
Furniture	$_____
Jewelry, furs, artwork	$_____
Sports and hobby equipment	$_____
Equity in your business	$_____
Total assets	$_____

Date_____

LIABILITIES

Unpaid bills	
Charge accounts	$_____
Taxes, property	$_____
Taxes, income	$_____
Rent or monthly mortgage	$_____
Balance due on	
Mortgage	$_____
Auto loan	$_____
Personal loan	$_____
Installment loan	$_____
College loan	$_____

Total liabilities $_____

After you've tallied up your assets (what you own) and listed your liabilities (what you owe) subtract liabilities from assets. The figure you arrive at is your net worth.

amazing how many people don't take time to do a budget or calculate their net worth.

Other documents that you will want to keep are:
- your savings book or statement records
- cancelled checks
- monthly statements from a money market deposit account
- CD statements
- savings bond records
- any tax returns you or your parents filed for you
- a copy of your Social Security card

Remember: making a mistake with money is not a disgrace unless you make the same mistake over and over again.

THE PRESIDENT'S NET WORTH

In June 1989, *Money* magazine estimated George and Barbara Bush's net worth at roughly $4 million. This places them in the top one percent of all U.S. households. Their single largest asset is a twenty-six-room house in Kennebunkport, Maine, which they purchased without a mortgage in 1981 for $800,000 from the President's aunt, Mary Walker. The property is estimated to be worth about $3 million.

Their other most valuable asset is a blind trust established when Bush became Vice President. On May 15, 1989, the White House said the trust was worth $998,000. The account is handled by the Bessemer Group, Inc., a New York City investment company.

Despite his hefty net worth and an annual salary of $200,000, President Bush is not a big spender. He buys his suits (Southwick and Norman Hilton) off the rack for between $400 and $600 and likes to eat at inexpensive restaurants where he keeps the bill to $20 per person. His reputation as a tipper? Only moderate.

George Bush's Maine estate.

Many students work to help pay high college costs.

11

MEETING COLLEGE COSTS

C ollege may seem a long way off, but September of freshman year will be here sooner than you think. And when it is, you and your family must be prepared to meet tuition bills. If you live on campus, you'll also face expenses for room and board. Add to that paying for transportation, books, clothes, and incidentals, and you have a hefty four-year bill.

The explosion in college costs has put students and parents on the alert. You can ease the way by planning well in advance. Even if your parents or grandparents plan to foot your tuition bill, you may be expected to cover the extras, such as books, getting to and from school, movies, and eating out. Each family's budget differs. Regardless of what your parent's financial situation is, your education will mean more to you if you pitch in and pay for part of it.

Setting Financial Goals

Setting financial-related goals makes saving a lot easier. It forces you to think about the amount of money involved and when it is needed. As your life changes, so will your goals; in fact, your goals should be revised on a regular basis.

When you set goals, write them in your budget notebook and assign each one a target date. One goal might be to pay for part of college. But your goals can be other things, such as starting up a business, buying your own car, helping your family, or taking a trip.

College Savings Tips

1) Make a list of several colleges you think you might like to attend. Write or call requesting information on tuition and financial aid. List the costs for each one in your budget notebook. Discuss it with your parents. Ask what they feel is possible. What will you be able to afford? What do they expect from you? How much can they contribute? Will you be doing it all on your own?

2) If you know you will need financial aid, begin gathering information now, or at least by the time you are a sophomore in high school. Check the list in the box on page 118.

3) If you must meet most of your expenses after high school, look into colleges with work-study programs so you can earn your way as you go.

4) Begin saving money now. Make it one of your goals to put aside a certain percentage of your allowance, gift money, or income from any jobs you have.

Ways to Save

In Chapter Eight we discussed Money Market Deposit Accounts and Certificates of Deposit.

THE RICHEST AMERICANS

Name	Residence	Net Worth	Business
John Kluge	Charlottesville, VA	$5.2 billion	Media
Samuel & Donald Newhouse	New York, NY	$5.2 billion	Publishing, cable TV
Barbara Cox Anthony Anne Cox Chambers	Atlanta, GA	$5.0 billion	Newspapers, TV, radio
Jay & Robert Pritzker	Chicago	$4.7 billion	Hotels, finance
Warren Buffett	Omaha, NE	$4.2 billion	Stock market
Sumner Redstone	Newton Center, MA	$2.88 billion	Cable TV
Ted Arison	Miami Beach, FL	$2.86 billion	Cruise ships
Ronald Perelman	New York, NY	$2.75 billion	Leveraged buyouts
Henry Ross Perot	Dallas, TX	$2.5 billion	Electronics

Source: The Forbes Four Hundred, Forbes *Magazine, October 23, 1989*

Review both of these sections. They are excellent places in which to stash your savings for college. Here are specific hints on using these and other investments for college:

• *Stagger CDs.* You recall that CDs have different lengths of maturity. If you purchase a CD that matures when you are ready for college, you will have that chunk of money available at that time. Try to buy four or more CDs, timed to come due each of the four years you are in college. Since there are penalties for cashing in CDs early, you won't be tempted to spend this money beforehand. (This is a good hint to share with your parents, who may be purchasing CDs.)

• *Buy Savings Bonds.* Congress passed a ruling affecting savings bonds purchased after January 1, 1990, that makes them ideal for certain families facing college costs. If used to pay tuition at qualified institutions, the bondholder will not have to pay any federal income tax on the interest the bonds earned. (Savings bonds are already free from state

GETTING HELP

Scholarships Not Based on Need
- Community groups
- Unions
- Trade associations

- Health professions

- Civic organizations
- Private corporations/businesses
- Art, athletic, academic scholarships
- National Merit scholarships

Grant and Loans
- Pell Grants
- Stafford Loans
- Supplemental Loans for Students (SLS)
- Parent Loans for Undergraduate Students (PLUS)

Financial Aid
- Check with any college you're interested in attending

and local income tax.) In order to get this tax break, you must meet the government's requirements:

1) The bonds must be held in your parent's name, not yours.

2) The bonds can only be used for tuition. Room and board and other expenses are not included.

3) Your family's income must not be above a certain level when the bonds are cashed in.

• *Buy Shares in a Money Market Mutual Fund.* Mutual funds have a savings-type account that is similar to a bank's money market deposit account. It is called a money market mutual fund. Although they are slightly less convenient to open than a bank account, they generally pay 1 to 2 1/2 percent more than the banks. They are extremely safe because they buy only high quality bonds and other short-term investments. The three funds listed below that are marked with an asterisk (*) consistently pay the highest yields. The other two pay lower interest rates but are listed because they are available to those who have less money on hand. Call the toll free numbers given below and ask the current interest rate and for an application. Invest your money in the fund that pays the most interest on the amount that you can afford to save. (*Note:* you will probably be required to have your parent's signature on your account.)

MONEY MARKET MUTUAL FUNDS

Fund Name	Minimum Investment	Telephone
*Alger Money Portfolio	$1,000	800-992-FUND
Colonial Government Trust	$250	800-225-2365
*Dreyfus Worldwide Dollar Money Fund	$2,500	800-645-6561
*Flex Fund	$2,500	800-325-FLEX
Twentieth Century Cash Reserve	no minimum	800-345-2021

APPENDIX

For More Ideas

Free publications

The College Planning Kit contains an excellent worksheet to help determine how much you will need by the time you reach college, how much to save each month, and whether the savings should be in your name or your parent's name.

T. Rowe Price
101 East Pratt Street
Baltimore, MD 21202
800-638-5660

Meeting College Costs
College Board Publications
P.O. Box 886
New York, NY 10101

Applying for Financial Aid
ACT Publications
P.O. Box 168
Iowa City, IA 52243

Books to Read

Don't Miss Out; The Ambitious Student's Guide to Scholarships and Loans by Robert and Ann Leider; Alexandria, VA: Octameron Associates, 1990.

The College Cost Book; New York: College Board Publications, 1989.

Video

How To Finance a College Education $45.75 (includes mailing)
   Campus Consultants, Inc.
   338 East 67th Street
   New York, NY 10021
   212-861-8806

Resolving Bank Problems

   If you have a question or a problem with a bank, first discuss it with a bank officer. If you need further help, contact one of the following agencies that regulates banking institutions.

   1. State Attorney General's Office
   (check your phone book for the address or call your library)
   This office maintains a complaint file and often can act quickly to resolve problems using state banking laws.

   2. If the bank is nationally chartered ("National" or the letters "N.A." will appear as part of the bank's name):

   U.S. Comptroller of the Currency
   Administrator of National Banks
   490 L'Enfant Plaza East, S.W.
   Washington, DC 20219
   202-447-1810

   3. If the bank is state chartered and a member of the Federal Reserve System, contact:

Board of Governors of the Federal Reserve System
Division of Consumer and Community Affairs
Federal Reserve Building
20th and C Streets, N.W.
Washington, DC 20551
202-452-3000

4. If the bank is state chartered and is insured by FDIC but not a member of the Federal Reserve System, contact:

Federal Deposit Insurance Corporation
Office of Bank Consumer Programs
550 Seventeenth Street, N.W.
Washington, DC 20429
800-424-5488 or 202-389-4221

5. For a problem with any stock or brokerage transaction a bank may have processed, contact:

Securities & Exchange Commission
450 Fifth Street, N.W.
Washington, DC 20549
202-272-2650

Things to Write Away For

• For a free copy of "The Bank Book," an informative brochure about all the services banks can offer customers, order brochure number 88500 from:

American Bankers Association
1120 Connecticut Avenue, N.W.
Washington, DC 20036
202-663-5987

• The Federal Reserve Banks publish fascinating brochures on money and banking. Here are some of the free publications available upon request. In addition, contact the bank in your area.

Public Information Department
Federal Reserve Bank of New York
33 Liberty Street
New York, NY 10045

"Coins and Currency"
"Federal Reserve: Cash on the Move"
"The Story of Money"

Public Information Department
Federal Reserve Bank of Atlanta
104 Marietta Street, N.W.
Atlanta, GA 30303-2713

"Don't Get Conned Out of Your Life Savings!"
"Electronic Funds Transfer"
"Federal Reserve Operations"
"Federal Reserve Structure"
"Fundamental Facts About U.S. Money"

Public Information Department
Federal Reserve Bank of Philadelphia
P.O. Box 66
Philadelphia, PA 19105-50066

"Endorsing Your Check"
"Options for Depositors"

• For information on visiting the U.S. Mint and an illustrated brochure of its history, contact:

The United States Mint
633 Third Street, N.W.
Washington, DC 20220

• For information about depositor's insurance, write or call for a free copy of "Your Insured Deposit," available from:

Federal Deposit Insurance Corporation
550 Seventeenth Street, N.W.
Washington, DC 20429
202-389-4221

• For more information on protecting your account, send $2.50 for a copy of "How Safe Is Your Money?" to:

Bank Rate Monitor
Box 088888
North Palm Beach, FL 33408
800-327-7717

INDEX

ACKNOWLEDGEMENTS AND PHOTO CREDITS

Pages 2, 40: Barbara Rios/Photo Researchers, Inc.; p. 8: Jerome Wexler/Photo Researchers, Inc.; pps. 11, 25, 27, 30, 39: The Bettmann Archive; p. 13: The Pierpoint Morgan Library, New York; p. 16: courtesy of Stacks Coin Company, New York; pps. 17, 37: Culver Pictures; p. 20–21: Pinkerton's, Inc.; pps. 22, 26, 29, 97: UPI/Bettmann Newsphotos; p. 31: Reuters/ Bettman Newsphotos; p. 34: Gerard Fritz/Monkmeyer Press; p. 45: David A. Krathwohl/Stock Boston; p. 50: Bob Daemmrich/Stock Boston; p. 59: Mahon/Monkmeyer Press; p. 64: courtesy of The Children's Bank; p. 65: Erika Stone/Photo Researchers, Inc.; p. 66: Mimi Forsyth/Monkmeyer Press; p. 69: Gary S. Weber/Photo Researchers, Inc.; p. 71: Springer/ Bettmann Film Archive; p. 72: Rameshwar Das/ Mankmeyer Press; p. 78: Bobbie Kingsley/ Photo Researchers, Inc.; p. 91: courtesy of Citicorp Diners' Club; p. 92: Erich Hartmann/ Magnum Photos, Inc.; p. 98: Paolo Koch/Rapho/Photo Researchers, Inc.; pps. 103, 113: AP/ Wide World Photos; p. 104: John F. Kennedy Library; p. 114: Peter Glass/Monkmeyer Press. Photo Research: Photosearch, Inc.